Windows
into the Lectionary

Also by the Author

Windows
into the Lectionary

Seasonal Anecdotes
for Preaching and Teaching

Donald L. Deffner

Resource Publications, Inc.
San Jose, California

Reprint Department
Resource Publications, Inc.
160 E. Virginia Street #290
San Jose, CA 95112-5876
1-408-286-8505 (voice)
1-408-287-8748 (fax)

Library of Congress Cataloging in Publication Data
Deffner, Donald L.
 Windows into the lectionary : seasonal anecdotes for preaching and teaching / Donald L. Deffner.
  p.   cm.
 Includes bibliographical references and index.
 ISBN 0-89390-393-0
 1. Homiletical illustrations. 2. Church year. I. Title.
 BV4225.2.D445 1996   96-42166

Editorial director: Kenneth Guentert
Prepress manager: Elizabeth J. Asborno
Copyeditor: Bonita Hurd

Printed in the United States of America

00 99 98 97 96 | 5 4 3 2 1

To my mentor
and father in Christ
Reuben W. Hahn,
pioneer
in the church's campus ministry

Contents

SEASONS OF ADVENT & CHRISTMAS

Advent

Christmas

Latter Sundays of Ordinary Time (Season after Pentecost)

Christ the King/Last Sunday of Ordinary Time (Season after Pentecost)

OTHER FEASTS & OCCASIONAL SERVICES

All Saints Day

Thanksgiving

Index of Themes

Index of Scripture References

Preface

The great English preacher Spurgeon once said:

> I hope to lend a handful of chips and shavings or, if you
> will, a bundle of firewood to a brother, with which he
> may kindle a fire on his own hearth and prepare food for
> his people. Possibly a lazy brother may boil his own pot
> with my sticks, but even that I shall not deplore so long
> as the food is well cooked (Fuller 9).

There is no intrinsic value in a sermon in which the preacher
did a good job of exegesis—or the teacher had a good lesson
plan—but failed to speak to the needs of the hearers. Communication involves more than just sound exposition of the
text or study of a lesson; it also means the use of imageries by
which people can apply the Biblical message to their lives.

Illustrations are "the windows that let in the light." This
means, broadly, any application of the "real Word to the real
world" of the hearer—not just a story, or humor (though
there's entirely too little of that in our preaching and teaching!).
The question to be asked is not "How can I use this illustration?" but, as I develop my material, "How is the Biblical truth
best illustrated here?" For our task is not to titillate the hearer
momentarily but to further intensify the applicability of *scrip-
tural* truth to the everyday life of the listener.

Our Lord was a master at the use of illustrations in his preaching and teaching. In Matthew 13:34 (TEV) we read: "He would not say a thing to them without using a parable." Christ always moved "from the known to the unknown." He dealt with the *real world* of the hearers, in the down-to-earth language of the marketplace, the farm, and the home.

"Consider the lilies, how they grow," he said (Lk 12:27). And the listener mentally responded: "Yes, Lord, why I was just watering my plants this morning!"

"A certain man was going down from Jerusalem to Jericho, when robbers attacked him" (Lk 10:30 TEV). Again the hearer reacted: "I know just what you're talking about, Lord! Why, a friend of mine was attacked on that road last week!"

Many sermons or study sessions fall short of their potential power in the lives of people today because they lack the principle Christ used in communicating: He did not talk *about* the Gospel; he used an illustration to apply it to life. His sermon or lesson was not an *idea discussed* but a *truth experienced.*

Bishop Gerald Kennedy once said: "People aren't tired of preaching. They're tired of *our* preaching.

This volume is offered to the preacher and teacher as one more aid in coming still closer to our Lord's model of preaching and teaching. It is hoped that on Sunday morning, as people come to receive the Bread of Life—and, "more abundantly," applied to their everyday living—that more and more they might say: "Lord, now with my own eyes I have seen your salvation....Now I can depart in peace" (paraphrase of Lk 2:29-30).

My above (adapted) preface introduced an earlier volume co-authored with Richard Andersen. It was titled *For Example: Illustrations for Contemporary Preaching.* To those principles I add the following "Criteria for the Use of Illustrations" taken from my *Compassionate Preaching:*

1. The illustration should flow from the text (or lesson) and its outline.

   Never make a theological point and then just "plunk in" an anecdote. That is an invalid illustration. Nor is the question (to repeat) "How can I use this excellent story I heard this week next time I preach or teach?" but rather "Where can I find a 'window to let in the light' on this particular point in the text or lesson?"

2. The illustration should not be remote from the world of the hearer but contemporary in application.

   I once heard a preacher remark, "We laugh when we see our children playing with paper hats and wooden swords." The reference must have been to the Crimean War from a book of illustrations published in 1895.

3. The illustration should not be apocryphal.

   This abstruse/obtuse type of illustration may try to make a theological point, but it is so fabricated or unreal that an intelligent listener can't believe it really happened at all.

   Take the supposed incident of the little boy who heard the preacher say we are to give ourselves *totally* to Jesus. So when the usher approached with the offering plate the boy asked the man to put the plate on the floor and he stepped inside it.

4. Avoid illustrations which sidetrack the listener.

   Eugene L. Lowry describes a sermon in which the student preaching recalled a marriage service he had conducted. In passing he stated that "the father of the bride arrived drunk." The student then made a sermonic point concerning a portion of the service he had conducted and went on to his next point. But the professor and the rest of the class were still wondering what had happened to the father. Did he make it through the whole service? While the preacher was on to his next point, the whole class was "still at the wedding—fantasizing what might have happened."

Lowry comments that he doesn't recall the next point in the sermon. "Such is the power of ambiguity and the necessity for closure" (Lowry 32-33.)

5. Strive for illustrations which are more than analogical.

Many illustrations fall flat because they make a theological *comparison* of sorts, but the analogy once made is lifeless and dull. Hosts of stories like this abound about pictures in museums. The preacher or teacher intones: "There is a picture in the Louvre," etc. etc. etc. "...and so it is in the Christian life...." Yuk! Ugh! So what! says the hearer. Tell me a story! (That's what Jesus did.) And that means...

6. Strive to select illustrations with a denouement ("denouement": the final revelation or occurrence which clarifies the nature and outcome of a plot).

As with the end of the sermon or lesson, communication will be much more powerful when there is the "hook," like the punch-line at the end of a well-told joke.

> The need for fellowship and cooperation in the church is
> the theme in the story of a little girl lost in a cornfield on
> a freezing winter day. Rescuers searched for her for
> hours, but to no avail. Finally one person suggested that
> the group start at one end of the field and, holding
> hands, traverse the field systematically. Finally, they
> found the child, but she was dead. The father,
> grief-stricken, cried out: "My God, why didn't we join
> hands before?"

7. The right use of humor in an illustration can further enhance communication.

This is a tricky one. We each have our own sense of humor (or lack of it). What is funny to one person can be consummately dull or offensive to another. So you must find your own way here. For example:

> When a ship was crossing a stormy bay, the engine suddenly stopped, and for a few minutes the situation was one of peril. A woman rushed up to the captain and asked anxiously, "Is there any danger?" "Madam," the captain replied, "we must trust in God." "Oh," she wailed, "has it come to that?" (Terrence E. Johnson, *Emphasis* 14, no. 4 [September 1, 1984]: 22).

Or this (titled *Large Diamond Pendant Came With Horrible Curse*, by Alex Thien [Green Bay Press Gazette, n.d.]):

> The Cruise Ship reached warm Jamaican waters and it was the night when dinner meant formal dress. At one table, a man noticed the woman next to him was wearing a diamond pendant. It was just about the biggest diamond he had ever seen.
>
> "I hope you don't mind my saying so, but that diamond is beautiful," he said.
>
> She smiled pleasantly.
>
> "I don't mind at all and thank you," she said. "It's the Klopman diamond."
>
> The guy looked puzzled.
>
> "I've heard of the Hope diamond and some others," he said, "but the Klopman is a new one to me."
>
> The lady explained the Klopman diamond was much like the Hope diamond, though somewhat smaller. However, the cuts were identical and it was equal in quality. The Klopman even came with a curse, the same as the Hope diamond.
>
> "That's astonishing—and it comes with a curse," mused the man.

The woman nodded. "If you'll forgive my curiosity, what kind of a curse?" he said.

"Mr. Klopman," she said.

With the above rubrics in mind, I present the illustrations in this book for your preaching and teaching. They are arranged according to the general themes implicit in the seasons of the church year. These topics are listed at the beginning of each section.

May the Lord bless not only the hearing but also the application of his Word to daily life—even as Jesus told stories.

The Church Year

Innumerable books are available to the preacher and teacher with respect to the church year. However, particularly because of the current trend away from the historic orders of the liturgy, a few additional words need to be said here. (Critical attention also needs to be given to the intrusion of subjective, sentimental "hymns" with banal lyrics which hardly express the reverent yet joyful affirmations of faith of the grand old hymns and chorales of the church.)

The preacher and teacher are to "contend for the faith which was once for all delivered to the saints" (Jude 3). The preacher and teacher also follow the *principle of retention* in contrast to those who discard the accreted liturgical heritage of the church. Accordingly, one is sensitive and faithful to the thematic flow of the church year and the practices of the church down through history.

The brief introductions at the beginning of each section are an attempt to "set the stage" for that season of the liturgical calendar.

Acknowledgments

Grateful acknowledgment is made for permission to reprint the following material:

Various passages are reprinted, with permission, from *More Telling Stories, Compelling Stories,* © 1993 by William J. Bausch, (paper, 188 pps, $9.95), published by Twenty-Third Publications, P.O. Box 180, Mystic, CT 06355. Toll free: 1-800-321-0411.

Various passages are reprinted, with permission, from *Timely Homilies: The Wit and Wisdom of an Ordinary Pastor,* © 1990 by William J. Bausch, (paper, 166 pps, $9.95), published by Twenty-Third Publications, P.O. Box 180, Mystic, CT 06355. Toll free: 1-800-321-0411.

Various quotations from *For Example* (1977), *Concordia Pulpit Resources* (journal, various issues), *The Concordia Pulpit* (various years), *Sermon Illustrations for the Gospel Lessons* (1980), and *Go and Make Disciples* (Jane Fryar, 1992), Copyright © Concordia Publishing House, Used by permission.

The Best of Your Life Is the Rest of Your Life, by Donald L. Deffner, copyright © 1977. Out of print.

Bold Ones on Campus, by Donald L. Deffner, copyright © 1973. Out of print.

Bound to Be Free, by Donald L. Deffner, copyright © 1981 Morse Press, Inc. Reprint © 1992 by Concordia Theological Seminary Press, Fort Wayne, Indiana 46825.

The Possible Years: Thoughts after Thirty on Christian Adulthood, by Donald L. Deffner, copyright © 1973. Out of print.

"Ship in Danger" from *Emphasis* (September 1, 1984) by Jerry Schmalenberger. Reprinted by permission from C. S. S. Publishing Co., Lima, Ohio.

Scripture quotations in this publication, except those cited otherwise, are from the New Revised Standard Version of the Bible, copyright 1989 by the division of Christian Education of the National Council of the Churches of Christ in the U.S.A., and used by permission.

Scripture quotations identified "TEV" are from Today's English Version text. Copyright © American Bible Society 1966, 1971, 1976. Used by permission.

Scripture quotations identified "NIV" are from the Holy Bible, New International Version. Copyright © 1973, 1978, 1984 by International Bible Society.

Scripture quotations identified "KJV" are from the King James or Authorized Version of the Bible.

I tender thanks to many friends who shared stories with me and applaud Pat Crawford for her usual outstanding work at the computer.

I also give plaudits to Kenneth Guentert and Elizabeth J. Asborno for their expertise in bringing the publication of this work to fruition.

SEASONS OF
ADVENT & CHRISTMAS

Advent

Advent—"coming"—is the preparatory season before Christmas. Therefore, such themes as readiness, watchfulness, and anticipation mark these days. But while this season is penitential, it is not as austere as the Lenten season.

Further, the accent of the Advent hope is on the coming of the King rather than on the coming of the kingdom. Although there is a sensitivity to the approach of the "end times," the lessons for the latter Sundays of the church year focus more intensively on that theme. Accordingly, illustrations dealing with death and the end of the world are placed in that section (see "Latter Sundays after Pentecost").

Christat the Apple Tree

Isaiah 11:1 "A shoot shall come out of the stump of Jesse"
Theme: Christ, the Coming

An anonymous eighteenth-century folk hymn is entitled
"Jesus Christ, the Apple Tree":

> The tree of life my soul hath seen,
> Laden with fruit and always green;
> The trees of nature fruitless be
> Compared with Christ the Apple Tree.
> His beauty doth all things excel;
> By faith I know, but ne'er can tell
> The glory which I now can see
> In Jesus Christ the Apple Tree.
> For happiness I long have sought,
> And pleasure dearly I have bought;
> I missed of all, but now I see
> 'Tis found in Christ the Apple Tree.
> I'm weary with my former toil,
> Here I will sit and rest awhile;
> Under the shadow I will be,
> Of Jesus Christ the Apple Tree.
> The fruit doth make my soul to thrive,
> It keeps my dying faith alive,
> Which makes my soul in haste to be
> With Jesus Christ the Apple Tree.

At first glance this work seems to be some sort of "new age"
music, incorporating at least the vestiges of nature worship,
pantheism, and anthropomorphism. But could this example
of floral symbolism be something else?

In medieval Europe "Adam and Eve Day" was celebrated
on December 24. On this day, ordinary people would act out
the story of Adam and Eve. Before the play began, however,
the actors would parade through town with Adam carrying the

Tree of Life on which apples were hung. By calling "Christ the Apple Tree," the author of this hymn identified Christ as the Second Adam. As one commentator put it:

> From the apparently dead and withered stump of Jesse shoots forth the green, supple new growth of a completely new being—the Second Adam, the Messiah, Jesus. Christ's birth itself is the real Christmas tree, the true Tree of Life being made incarnate in our world....Christ incarnates the Tree of Life and brings the possibility of eternal life back to all humanity. Through Christ, the Second Adam, death itself will die, finally relinquishing its icy grip from humanity's throat.

This month as you prepare for the coming of the Christ Child, remember the "tree of life," the new, tender shoot sprouting from the stump of Jesse. As you choose your fir, spruce, or pine Christmas tree, remember all other trees are nothing compared to the fruit-laden "Apple Tree" of Christ. As you view the many beautiful and lavish Christmas decorations in homes and businesses, remember that it is only faith that grasps the beauty and glory of "Jesus Christ the Apple Tree." As you search high and low for that perfect gift to make someone happy, remember that all happiness and pleasure are found in "Jesus Christ the Apple Tree." As you weary of the hectic pace, experience the triviality, and sense the loneliness evident in this season, remember "Jesus Christ the Apple Tree" provides an oasis of shade, a place of rest. As you long for spiritual rebirth, remember that the fruit of this tree makes the soul healthy, keeps faith alive, and makes you long to be with "Jesus Christ the Apple Tree."

David Owren

"I Know I'm Playing with Fire"

Matthew 24:44 "You also must be ready"

Theme: Readiness

Many times we fail to take Jesus' warning seriously. "He is coming back, but we have things to do first." "He won't come back today or tonight; after all, it has been almost two thousand years since Jesus lived and judgment day has not come yet." "What are the chances, anyway?"

I made an evangelism call on a man, a locksmith by trade, around forty years old as I recall. He was polite and listened as we told to him the Gospel of our Lord Jesus. We told him that salvation was by grace alone and you could not earn or deserve it. We told him that Jesus died to pay the price for all the wrongs that all men had done in their lives. Jesus had won for him a place in heaven and offered it to him as a free gift. He was invited to believe this Gospel. He mused for a moment and said, "No, I don't think so." He proceeded to explain, "I know that I am playing with fire here, but you see, I'm having a lot of fun right now, and I don't want to give that up just yet. I like to hit the bars and I have a couple of girlfriends on the side. So I think I'll say no, and I may not wait till I'm eighty. But a few more years of this fun is for me."

Do we ever think like him? Have we ever? "It doesn't matter what I do today as long as I don't get caught."

The issue is not whether someone on the outside catches us. What are we like on the inside? What do we really believe about the grace of God? ·

Robert Mikkelson

"Here He Comes!"

Mark 13:35 "You do not know when (he)...will come"
Theme: Readiness

I was an elementary school teacher for twenty-four years. I was blessed with those years of experience and the service in the kingdom. Dealing with children on a consistent basis is a real study in human nature as a whole. Each class made up of individuals also takes on its unique character as a whole as they relate to one another, their teacher, and their tasks as students. Students reveal their new nature in Christ and also their sinful nature over the course of a year.

One way a teacher can get to know the class rather quickly is to leave the room for a few minutes. This happens from time to time when the teacher must take a phone call or talk to a parent in the office. I would usually say, "Please continue on your assignment and I will be back in a few minutes."

There were basically three different class types when it came to students' regard to the task at hand. One class type was many times in trouble when the teacher was in the room. The teacher had to always be alert to trouble brewing. Consequently, when the students were left to fend for themselves for a while, all constraints were off and you could hear them all over the building.

The second class type was made up of basically responsible students, but they could be mischievous and sometimes devious. You could rarely hear them in the hallway when the teacher was out of the room, but upon return the teacher would turn the corner in the hallway and hear the loud whisper of a student saying, "Here he comes! Here he comes!" By the time the teacher walked into the room everyone was in their seat and most were pretending to be working.

The third type of class was most always trustworthy. When they were left on their own for a time they most times stayed in their seats and finished their work. And unless they were unattended for a really long period of time, they still were productive.

Yes, there are times that this really does happen. I, as principal, at one time was taking a new parent through the school and we came upon the third and fourth grade room. All was quiet and hardly a head turned from work to acknowledge that we were there. Needless to say, the new parent *did* take notice.

Jesus will return and he left us with tasks to accomplish. What is our attitude about those tasks? What is our attitude about our Lord and his return? Which class are we like as individuals and as a group? Do we forget that God is coming back? Does it make a difference in our lives?

Robert Mikkelson

The Greatest Sin on Campus

Matthew 24:44 "You also must be ready"
Theme: Readiness

At the University of Wisconsin, campus Pastor Ed Wessling immediately had the student congregation in the palm of his hand. He began:

"Today I want to speak about the greatest sin on this university campus…"

The chapel was hushed.

"The greatest sin on this campus," he continued, "is not beer or sex."

You could hear a pin drop.

"The greatest sin on this campus is not beer or sex, but…"

Three hundred and fourteen heads leaned forward in anticipation.

"…the greatest sin on this campus is *procrastination!*"

The Silver Platter

Matthew 24:44 "You also must be ready"
Theme: Readiness

When I was a senior in high school one of my teachers explained his philosophy regarding tests on the material being read in our studies. He called his philosophy "The Silver Platter Testing Policy." He would hand us an exact copy of the test to be taken in one week. We could use our textbook to find the answers to the questions and then use that as a study guide. He assured us that the actual test would be just what he claimed it to be. He wanted everyone to do well in his class; and if we put forth the effort, we could get an A handed to us on a silver platter, an actual platter from his home.

My grade for the first test was a C. The teacher asked me, "What happened? Why only a C?" I explained that I had not left myself enough time to study for the test, that I was busy playing baseball, surfing, and watching too much TV. I had put off studying until it was *too late.*

On the next two tests I received A's handed to me on the silver platter. But I had no one to blame but myself for the C on the first test.

My final grade for the course was a B+. My excuses for not doing better were pathetic and I got just what I deserved—no more, no less.

From the very beginning of history, God has offered us hope, peace, joy, and eternal life, all on a "Silver Platter."

He owes us nothing yet he clothes us in his righteousness and gave his own Son to die for us that we may have life with him and have it abundantly. His love is served on a "Silver Platter," in the form of a cross. When Jesus died on the cross our sins died with him and as he was raised from the dead we too have been raised to eternal life.

Howard Barth

"Talking for 2,000 Years"

John 2:3 "The wine gave out"
Theme: Readiness

You can imagine what in all likelihood happened at the wedding at Cana when it was announced to the bride and groom that they were out of wine. Now the steward of the feast had responsibility to oversee the feast, but the shame of such an oversight in a land where hospitality is so highly regarded would have, without a doubt, been born for years by the family.

A wife in 30 A.D. would probably not have responded exactly like a wife in the 20th century, but the message to the groom would have been the same. Can't you just hear the bride say in shock and disbelief, "We're out of wine? How could this happen? It was your responsibility to see that there was enough of everything. Who came here anyway that drank so much that we would run out? Who was to monitor the consumption? You know that drunkenness is a sin and a disgrace on us. Who came that was not invited? Did you invite those followers of Jesus? Now what will we do that our wedding is ruined? We're a disgrace! People will probably talk about us for the next 2,000 years!"

Robert Mikkelson

"Beans and Jell-O"

John 2:3 "The wine gave out"
Theme: Readiness

In 1985 my family and I attended the Goetch family reunion. They are the family on my mother's side and they hold a reunion at fairly regular intervals. They are a large family, and they now hail from all corners of the earth but mainly from Wisconsin, Minnesota, and Iowa. The committee met. The festivities were planned. Six hundred and fifty people were to attend, so the gathering was to be held in the Youth Hall of Marathon Park in Wausau, Wisconsin. And Patricia Goetch/ Bordan, the family genealogist, was to be selling her newly published book containing the family tree. The names of all the Goetches over the age of one year were contained in this book, which might account for the 650 people in attendance. The book was called *Roots and Branches,* and sold for $12.

Now the Goetches are a frugal lot and carefully watch where their money goes, unless it goes to something you can drive or it buys something that comes in a bottle or a can. With the large outlay of expense for this shindig, the committee decided to keep the cost of the registration down and to have a potluck meal—a good idea, because all those Goetches were of sturdy farm background and all have put on a feed in their day.

The day of the reunion came, and all filed in with their assorted dishes and put them on a long row of tables along the west wall of the Youth Building. Since the afternoon would be long and the food would soon get cold, the table prayer was led by Pastor Goetch and the tables were dismissed one at a time to go up for their food starting with those on the west end, closest to the food.

We were sitting on the east side of the hall. It took a long while to feed the large group and by the time our line of tables of 150 people reached the food, all that was left was *beans* and *Jell-O. They ran out of all the good stuff.*

Beans and *Jell-O! Beans* and *Jell-O!* We took what we thought we could stand and wove our way back through the tables of the now full and contented Goetches. There were gray-haired Grandma Goetches in print dresses sitting at their places with their hands in their laps and their napkins crumpled on their empty plates. Middle-aged men with round stomachs and suspenders leaning back sucking on toothpicks. Chunky, teenaged girls still finishing their last piece of cake.

Strapping big boys still sitting in front of plates piled high with chicken bones. And a bunch of little Goetches all running around between the tables leaving their plates half full of casserole and potato salad.

Let me tell you, those 150 people were not happy campers! *And the committee heard about it too, for many years. There was not enough.* All that careful planning still had flaws and foul-ups, and the tongues they did wag.

Did you ever plan carefully and still have your plans come to naught?

Robert Mikkelson

The Stealthy Burglar

Philippians 4:4 "Rejoice in the Lord always"
Theme: Rejoicing

The man in the shadows waited pretty much until the family got all of its belongings into the car, checked everything, had the car loaded up, and pulled away for their summer vacation. The man in the shadows waited until it was dark and then he went to the front door of the house and range the bell. When there was no answer, this man, seasoned burglar that he was, had no trouble picking the lock and getting inside. As a precaution he called out into the darkness, "Is anybody home?" and he was stunned when he heard a voice reply, "I see you, and Jesus sees you."

Terrified, the burglar called out, "Who's there?" And again the voice came back, "I see you, and Jesus sees you." So the burglar switched on his flashlight, turned it toward the direction of the voice, and was immediately relived to see a caged parrot who recited once more, "I see you, and Jesus sees you." He laughed to himself and then went to the wall and threw on the wall switch. Then he saw it. Beneath the parrot's cage was a huge Doberman pinscher. Then the parrot said, "Attack, Jesus, attack!"

It's good to laugh out loud, because as you attended to that second reading, you heard St. Paul start out by saying, "Rejoice! Have joy!" And even though there's a lot to be said about the possibility of war, recession, and a whole litany of troubles that daily press in on us human beings, we are nevertheless invited on this Third Sunday of Advent to laugh a little and rejoice.

William J. Bausch, *More Telling Stories*, 32-33

Christmas

Christmas, with Easter and Pentecost, is one of the three great mountain peaks of the Christian church year. Do you find it as difficult as I do to find fresh material for preaching and teaching during those joyous, sacred days?

At this time the novice speaker does well to avoid another re-run against commercialism, or make disparaging remarks about Christmas parties, or rant against Santa Claus—"the bibulous glutton dressed in a red suit, uttering innocuous phrases like 'Merry X-mas!' and 'Season's Greetings!'" Our people have heard those comments many times before.

Nor do we trivialize Christmas by telling children we are going to "have a birthday party for Jesus." A sword was to pierce his mother's heart (Lk 2:35). This babe was born to die on a cross...*for us.*

Better the spirit and the exalted prose of O. P. Kretzmann, president of Valparaiso University (*Campus Commentary*, c. 1967):

> Our Christmas in 1967 was a very happy one...happy
> because the Child gave us the power to see its
> meanings...because in spite of sin and suffering the
> world is lovely, for he came to live with us, and his feet
> have trodden the earth...because in our hearts winter is
> now past, the rain is over and gone, and the flowers

have appeared in the land...because the manger is not an end, but a beginning...the beginning of Christmas here always until the end when the day breaks and the shadows retire...because he, the Child and Holy One, can wipe away all tears from our eyes...even with hands smaller than yours....May God give us a clean heart and a sure faith at Christmas.

The Angels of Christmas

Luke 2:10 "The angel said to them"
Theme: Christmas

Without angels, the first Christmas would have been a very puzzling series of events.

Without an angel, Elizabeth (who was the mother of John the Baptist) would have become pregnant with no explanation how and with no information as to the name and purpose of her special child.

Without an angel, Mary would not have known how she got pregnant. She would never have known that her child was the Son of God. She would not have been able, later, to follow her son and submit to him in faith.

Without an angel, Joseph would have never married the virgin mother. He would have "divorced her secretly," as the Bible says. Mary would probably not have gone to Bethlehem since she would have stayed in Nazareth with her family. So the Savior may well have not been born in Bethlehem and the Bible would not have been fulfilled.

Without an angel, Mary never would have known what to name her child. She might have named him Heli after her father or maybe Shealtel or Matthat. Whoever heard of a savior named Shealtel? Of course, without angels, Mary wouldn't have known her son was a savior.

Without angels, even if Mary had gone to Bethlehem, there would have been no shepherds visiting the tiny infant. No one would have known that the infant son of Mary was also Christ the Lord. We'd have no "joy," no "peace," no "Good News," no "glory," since all these Christmas words were given by the mouths of angels. The first Christmas would be boring.

Worse yet, without an angel Joseph would not have known of King Herod's wicked plan to kill the newborn baby. Mary and child would not have fled to Egypt and the poor baby would have died along with all the other little boys of

Bethlehem. So the Savior would have died thirty years too soon. And, if by chance Mary and Joseph had escaped to Egypt, they would probably have stayed there since no one would have told them to go back to the land of Israel.

Without angels, Christmas would never have happened.

The word *angel* means messenger. God has always used messengers to spread the good news. Sometimes angels are heavenly. More often they are people from this world who share the news of Christmas, "Glory to God in the highest and on earth, peace—good will—to men."

Klemet Preus

"Forgive Us Our Christmases"

Luke 2:11 "To you is born...a Savior"
Theme: Christmas

Particularly at Christmastime, with the dither and the bustle of all the preparation, our lives can be darkened by impatience, or bickering, or rough words, all of which are far from the peaceful and gentle spirit Christ wants us to have.

For example, in one home on Christmas Eve there was a lot of noise and activity. The father was busy with all sorts of packages and last minute chores. The mother's nerves were frayed and had reached the breaking point several times. Their one small daughter was constantly in the way no matter what she did. Finally, she was simply sent off to bed with harsh words and a hasty "good night!"

As she prayed alone the Lord's Prayer before going to sleep, all the high-pitched tension of the day took its toll. The little girl's mind was somewhat mixed up when she came to the middle of the prayer, and she said: "and forgive us our Christmases, as we forgive those who Christmas against us" (adapted from Wolber 28).

"Forgive us our Christmases"! How often we need to pray that. Either because we don't really care enough about making peace for others in the world—or even in our own homes. Often there is no real peace in our hearts because we have not really cared enough—and wanted Christ enough to come—to dispel the darkness in our hearts. We have often wanted to remain in the dark, as if Christ had never been born. For that we need to repent. And because of that, Christ needs to be *re*born in our lives, *every day*.

"Christmas Frees from Chains"

Luke 2:10 "Good news of great joy"
Theme: Christmas

Christmas is upon us. What a wonderful time of year. Hearts are open and homes are warm with the smell of the season. Decorations have been displayed since who knows when, and gifts are being wrapped and mailed or stored under a tree.

The other day, I took the family to a grand performance of Dickens's *A Christmas Carol*. Again the message hit home, but not as I expected.

It was early in the production, after Scrooge has proven himself to be of sufficiently hard heart to forgo any seasonal sentiment. Marley's ghost has made its entrance and is engaging a sleepy-eyed Scrooge in foreboding dialogue. That's when it happened. I heard a line which sounded so true, so much like the warning of the season.

It must have been something I ate or the rush-rush bad mood left over from the morning madness. The line didn't settle in quite right. Could I be hearing what I was hearing?

Could it really be true? Do I have to live in the confines of the chain I forge link by link?

"I wear the chain I forged in life," Marley warns Scrooge. "I made it link by link, and yard by yard. I girded it on of my own free will, and of my own free will wear it."

I thought Christmas was about warm, fuzzy feelings that set aside everyday cynicism and economic consideration for a while. I thought if I bought the kids a few of the things on their list and got the wife a new sweater, everything would be all right.

The thought haunted me while I sat and watched. I saw myself in Christmas past and the opportunities I had missed. I saw myself in Christmas present, ignoring some much-needed kindness. I saw myself at Christmas and wondered of the coming years. Nothing much had changed in days gone by. Christmas was as wearisome as ever. Come the relief of January, would I go back to life as usual?

Then it happened again—Scrooge's question of the spirit of Christmas yet to come. "Are these the things which must be or are these the things that may be?" Is there truly the possibility of change?

Scrooge woke up, but I went home in turmoil. It is true! The grave is the end. So what if Scrooge had a couple of years to campaign for a big flowery funeral? What then? Who would remember him after he was gone? How could he possibly reverse the damage done in three- or four-score years of uncaring heritage? The spirit of Christmas yet to come had no answer. Now I had none as well.

I wandered on into the evening and fell restlessly asleep. Thank goodness for the sunshine of morning. The light of a new day was sure to be shed on the dilemma in my spirit. My hope was not fruitless.

The words of the angels were welcome assurance as I worshiped anew the God I thought I knew. "Peace on earth, good will to those who are favored by God." That's it! I'm not sure about the peace on this earth, but in my world there is peace this Christmas.

Now I know the ghost was wrong. "It is required of every man that the spirit within him should walk abroad among his fellow-men, and travel far and wide; and if that spirit does not go forth in life, it is condemned to do so after death."

Now I am again sure the season is one of joy. I sing the carols heartily with my fellow believers. I know the reason for the season!

God has provided an escape from a life of dreadful confinement in chains of error. My savior was born just like me. He lived the life I could never live. He died the punishment I deserved. He lives now as the assurance that I am forgiven and set free.

Christmas is God's gift to me. No chains please—only a savior for me.

Adapted from Peter Kolb

Is There Room in Your Heart?

Luke 2:7 "There was no place for them in the inn"
Theme: Christmas

Tom was fourteen years old and big for his age— physically. But mentally he was about four—educationally impaired. Nevertheless he had faithfully attended Sunday school for years and knew that Jesus was his Savior.

In the Christmas pageant Tom had only one line. He was the innkeeper, and all he had to say was "There is no room" when Mary and Joseph came to the inn looking for a place to stay.

Tom practiced his line for weeks, until he could open the door, listen to Joseph's request, and then in a strong voice proclaim, "There is no room."

The night of the pageant came. Everyone was dressed in their authentic costumes. One young girl played the pregnant Mary. Her face was glowing with joy. A lad dressed as Joseph tried to look mature and responsible.

The two came down the aisle of the church and knocked at the door of the "inn." Tom swung the door open, and on cue responded, "There is no room."

But at that point Tom didn't understand that it was a play. As Mary and Joseph turned to walk away, tears ran down his face. Suddenly he called out to them "Wait! Don't go! You can have my room!"

"A quiet manger kept for Thee…"

Ed Parker

"No Hell! No Hell!"

Luke 2:11 "To you is born…a Savior"
Theme: Christmas

The Sunday school was completing their Christmas pageant rehearsal. The children's part was to climax with their spirited singing of the carol with the words "Noel, Noel! Born is the King of Israel."

The children were singing joyfully enough, but the teacher still sensed that something was not quite right. He looked carefully at the choir, listening and then he caught it.

It was little Megan, the loudest one, who had mixed up the words. Her happy song was "No hell, no hell! Born is the King of Israel."…

(Christ *has*) come to suffer your worst pain, worst distress, worst humiliation. He has taken away the punishment due for your and my sin. He is God's great Christmas gift, given us to hang on a tree. Not some pretty Christmas tree. He is born for a tree stripped bare, made of rougher wood—the cross of Calvary…

Greet God. Your savior. From your wrongs, he is the rescue. No hell, no hell! Born is the King of Israel. Christ, your savior, is born. Christ, your savior is born!

Adapted from Stephen Gaulke

What's in Your Barn?

Luke 2:10 "I am bringing you good news"
Theme: Christmas

Maurice Wright was a British farmer who bought a large painting from a neighboring farmer for less than $4. He hung the painting in his barn. After collecting cobwebs for several years, it was noticed by the farmer's tax accountant. Wondering what it was worth, he took a color photo of the painting and sent it to Christie's, the well-known London auction firm. He learned that the painting was done by Thomas Daniell, a highly acclaimed nineteenth-century artist. The painting turned out to be an 1808 Daniell. Art critics were aware of its existence, but it had come to be known as the "Lost Daniell," its whereabouts a mystery for over a century. Farmer Wright sold the painting at an auction for more than $90,000. Imagine finding something like that in your barn!

The Good News of this season is that a priceless treasure is born in a barn—Christ, your savior. He brings you forgiveness for sins, new life now, and eternal life for the future. You can't put a price tag on the value of that gift. And you don't have to, because this gift is free for you and for all people. Jesus Christ should not be like a treasure hidden in the barn of your life. He should be brought out into the open so all can see and appreciate the priceless treasure of his salvation.

"I bring you good news of great joy that will be for all the people."

David W. Hoover

Epiphany

Epiphany—"appearance" or "manifestation"—celebrates our Lord's salvation for *all* people. He is a "Light to lighten the Gentiles."

Accordingly, the theme of *evangelization* (a dynamic process, not "evangelism," a topic) is highlighted at this time. And, as J. Russell Hale puts it, "The *raison d'être* (reason for being) of the Church is *evangelization*." And this does not mean only talk *about* "foreign" missions but outreach to the "Gentiles" in our own back yard. Illustrations on witnessing are collected in this section.

"Do You Believe That Stuff?"

Acts 4:13 "When they saw [their] boldness...they were amazed"
Theme: Boldness/Confidence

The one agnostic was puzzled as he said to his fellow doubter, "Why do you go to hear that fellow preach all the time? You don't believe the stuff that he says, do you?"

"No," said his friend in reply, "but he does."

The preacher they were referring to was unashamed of preaching the Gospel of Jesus Christ. Yet it was not a Gospel of his own making, nor did he have a power from within himself that caused the one doubter to come back again and again to hear what he had to say. We recall the example in the Book of Acts when two of our Lord's disciples were fulfilling the missionary calling with which the Lord had entrusted them, and the Scripture says: "Now when they saw the boldness of Peter and John and perceived that they were uneducated, common men, they wondered; and they recognized that they had been with Jesus" (Acts 4:13).

Donald L. Deffner, *Bold Ones on Campus,* 150

"Christ Isn't Here Today"

Galatians 3:27 "You...have clothed yourselves with Christ"
Theme: Christ-likeness

A Christian couple planned to sell their home to a black physician and his wife. They received threatening phone calls from their neighbors. One said, "How could you do this to us?"

The Christian woman selling the home said, "We're simply doing what Christ would do."

But her irritated caller responded, "But he isn't here today!"

Christ isn't here today?

Christ *is* here today—in you and in me as baptized and redeemed children of God. When we catch the mind of Christ and by the power of the Holy Spirit put on his character and traits and likeness, we *do* learn to live daily with thankfulness and expectation. We *do* make his very presence known by the way in which we live among other people.

Donald L. Deffner, "How Do You Start Your Day?"
Concordia Pulpit for 1987, 2

Real-Life Mission Work

Matthew 9:38 "Ask...the Lord...to send out laborers"
Theme: Missions

It looks so easy in the movies!...or on TV...or in all those inspirational mission books. The missionary, full of enthusiasm and on fire for the Lord, hacks his way through the jungle, stumbles upon a village of half-naked natives, quickly learns their language, shares the Gospel, and is suddenly surrounded by the joyous smiles of the whole village, forever indebted to him for bringing them the Good News that they have awaited for the last few thousand years.

The whole village is immediately baptized, and they pour themselves into the Scriptures, which the missionary has graciously given to them in their own language. And they, in their excitement, run to all the neighboring villages (like the Samaritan woman at the well) telling everyone in their path the Good News. Before long, the whole country is converted. Little congregations are everywhere, and the villages have their own pastors and are sending out their own missionaries. As in the time of the Pentecost where three thousand believed from one sermon by Peter, the Holy Spirit is active, and the church is exploding.

Our missionary friend smiles, says a prayer of thanks, thinks of what John the Baptist said ("He must increase, and I must decrease"), turns and walks into the setting sun and toward another field where the harvest is also white for the reaping.

It looks so easy in the movies, on TV, or in books…but then that is fantasy and this is reality. And the reality is that while there are still plenty of villages in remote places that have never heard the Gospel, the bulk of the harvest is not in the jungles but in the cities. While remote villages can be exotic, the air there crisp and clean, and the beauty of nature at hand, the cities of the world are pretty much the same everywhere… jam-packed full of people. And it is to people that the Gospel must be brought.

The sense of community that would tend to bind the people of a village together is drowned in the sea of human individuality that swirls within a city. So people must be reached individual by individual, family by family, and it is a slow process. Learning another language is a hard, slow process, but getting to know people in a city is even more painstaking—but that is the secret: getting to know them, living with them, understanding their joys and sorrows, and letting them know yours.

And then, after a while, a Bible study finally gets rolling along, then dwindles out. And the missionary tries again, maybe with another family…and again, and again. And eventually there is a group who want to be baptized and receive the Lord's Supper: a congregation!

And ever so slowly, leaders may begin to emerge…then disappear. Some have a job change, a move to another city or back to the country…and hopefully, they take their newfound, fragile zeal with them, and the church continues to grow without, and in spite of, the best laid plans of the missionary.

But the missionary worries: are they ready to strike out on their own yet? And what about the vacuum in the struggling little congregation, created by their departure? And the missionary is forced once again to allow the Holy Spirit the ultimate responsibility of raising up the church.

The passing of time is one of the biggest frustrations for the missionary. Like John the Baptist, the missionary may not live to see the glory of the Pentecost and the explosive work of the Holy Spirit. The missionary may see only the first humble beginnings and may wonder, as did the Baptist, if these humble beginnings are all that are to be or if, indeed, God has even greater things in store.

But then come the comforting words of Jesus: "Go and tell John the things which you hear and see: The blind receive their sight and the lame walk; the lepers are cleansed and the deaf hear; the dead are raised up and the poor have the Gospel preached to them."

Jesus is not here in the flesh performing miraculous healings now, but if the missionary looks closely, though the visible number of converts seems small and the years long, he can see the spiritually blind receive their sight, the ears of the spiritually deaf opened, the spiritually dead raised, because all of them, destitute in sin, are having the Gospel preached to them.

And the missionary knows that even in this reality of slow tedious work riddled with disappointments, the Word of the Lord will not return to him empty but will accomplish his will and purpose. And he has the great joy and privilege of being used by his savior to preach this Word to the poor. And he is also privileged to see some of the first buds spring forth from the seeds that he has planted...

And he smiles and offers up a prayer of thanks.

Nicholas D. Wirtz, at a mission station in Panama

The Ever-Fresh Rosebud

John 4:14 "The water that I will give...will become...eternal life"
Theme: Witnessing

Dr. Howard Kelly, famed surgeon of Baltimore and re-
nowned for the Christian principles he maintained in his
profession, was seldom seen without a beautiful rosebud in
the lapel of his coat. It remained fresh for a long time—and
there was a reason. When people asked him the secret, he
turned the lapel and showed them a little glass vial containing
water. The stem of the rose went through the buttonhole into
the water and thus was kept fresh for a longer time. Dr. Kelly
would then tell inquirers that the secret of beautiful and
fragrant Christian living lies in drawing refreshment from the
water of life, Jesus Christ.

Wilbur E. Nelson, 44

"It Wasn't Luck at All"

Acts 4:20 "We cannot keep from speaking"
Theme: Witnessing

A young mother was alone with her three children on a
remote farm in central California. The three children had been
swimming in their pool, when she suddenly noticed that the
two-and-a-half-year-old was at the bottom of the pool. She got
the child out as quickly as she could, and just then a
neighboring farmer came by. He immediately began the
tedious and fearful process of mouth-to-mouth resuscitation
to try to save the child. After seven minutes life stirred in the
little form; and the doctors said, after a later examination, they
were sure there had been no brain damage.

In the days following, people who heard of the child's rescue from drowning would comment to the father or mother: "You sure were *lucky!*" "You sure were *lucky!*" But the father told his pastor, "When people would say that to me, I replied, 'It wasn't luck at all. My wife and daughter were on their knees praying while our friend was working on my son.' " And he concluded, "What a wonderful opportunity I had for witnessing to Christ again and again as my friends spoke to me about my son being saved."

"For we cannot stop speaking of what we ourselves have seen and heard" (Acts 4:20 TEV).

Donald L. Deffner, "God's Message—Man's Salvation,"
Concordia Pulpit for 1976, 105

"They Never Caught On"

Matthew 5:16 "Let your light...shine before [others]"
Theme: Witnessing

A college student was chatting with a friend of his about his coming job in the north woods. His friend said, "I wonder if you really know what you're letting yourself in for. That's a pretty rough lot of men up there."

When the summer had passed, the two friends met again. The one asked the other: "Well, how did you, *a Christian,* make out with that crowd?"

"Oh," said the other, "I didn't really have any trouble. *They never caught on!*"

Donald L. Deffner, *The Possible Years*, 56

"You Tell Her, Billy!"

Matthew 5:16 "Let your light shine before others"
Theme: Witnessing

(*This story sounds almost too good to be true, but it is true. Even the dialogue is about ninety percent as originally spoken. Although it took place more than forty years ago, it was so powerful an experience as to be imprinted indelibly on my memory.*)

I hadn't been in my first parish long before I knew we had a problem. This was a struggling little old congregation on New York's Lower East Side which had been in decline for more than fifty years, but decline was not the problem I refer to. The problem was a six-year-old by the name of Billy. He did not come to Sunday school often, but when he came it was a disaster. Billy was nothing but trouble. He never listened, or so we thought. He disrupted his class constantly—punching the other students, leaving his place, talking out loud in inappropriate ways. He was the despair of his teacher. No one knew what to do about him. We were relieved on those Sundays when he didn't show up.

Billy did not have much going for him. He was from a very poor and broken home. He was malnourished and somewhat crippled. He had a nervous twitch. All this was in addition to and, no doubt, contributing to his obnoxious personality. He lived in a tenement apartment about a mile from the church and parsonage, across many very busy streets.

Late one afternoon about the time rush hour traffic was at its peak, my doorbell rang. When I answered it I was surprised to see Billy there, holding the hand of a little girl about his age. "Billy," I asked, "what are you doing here?"

"This is my friend Celia, Pastor. She doesn't know anything about Jesus, so I brought her here so that you could tell her about him."

I could hardly believe my ears. Billy, whom we thought never listened or cared, brought his little friend all that way across some of the busiest streets in the world so that he could introduce her to Jesus. I invited them in and sat them down. What I said next without even thinking about it surprised me almost as much as what Billy said. ...

"Billy," I said, "you know about Jesus. Why don't you tell her about him." To my astonishment, Billy replied without any hesitation and with complete confidence.

"Celia, Jesus was the nicest person who ever lived. He was so good to everyone. If they were sick, he would make them well. If they were hungry, he would feed them. If they were sad, he would cheer them up. He was so nice. But some bad people hated him, and one day they caught him and they hurt him and they killed him."

"I think I heard about that once," Celia interrupted. "They stuck arrows in him, didn't they?" (Probably she was thinking of the spear.)

"But, you know what? He didn't have to let them do that," Billy quickly added. "He wasn't just a man. He was God, too, and he could have stopped them. But he let them do it anyway, and you know why Celia? He did it for us, so that God would not have to punish us for the bad things that we do."

Deeply moved, Celia responded, "Aw, he shouldn't have done that."

"But he didn't stay dead," Billy explained excitedly. "Three days later he came back to life again. He went to see his friends, and were they ever glad to see him. Then, after a while, he went back to heaven again, but you know what, he's still here anyway. We can't see him, but he's here all the time. And, when we're good it really makes him happy, and when we're bad, it makes him sad. And someday, Celia, he's going to come back from heaven and we will be able to see him, and he's going to take us to heaven to be with him forever. Isn't that wonderful?"

Poor little disturbed and obnoxious Billy, who never seemed to listen in Sunday school or to care about the Lord, was deeply concerned about his friend and her need for the Lord, and he did something about it. Despite all of his personal limitations and problems, he gave the most beautiful witness I have ever heard. We often feel inadequate when the time comes for us to speak up for our savior. But one thing is sure—if Billy could do it, so can we.

Milton L. Rudnick

"The Woman at the Well? That's *Me!*"

1 Peter 3:15 (NIV) "Always be prepared to give an answer"
Theme: Witnessing

Dr. Eugene Bunkowske, missiologist, tells of the following incident which occurred when he boarded a plane for a brief trip to Chicago.

"The plane was not full, and as I came down the aisle I was tempted to take one of the many empty seats. I had much work to do, and I would have enjoyed a little privacy. But the Holy Spirit seemed to say to me: Take your assigned seat.

"As I introduced myself to the woman next to me, I did not say I was a clergyman. That often turns people off immediately and ends conversation. I said I was a missionary, and she immediately opened up. She spoke of a recurring, inexplicable dream which she had had since she was a child, and as we talked I sensed the clear opportunity to present the Gospel to her.

"I started with John 4, the story of the woman at the well of Sychar, who had had several husbands. Immediately the woman, whose name was Angela, identified with the woman in the text. 'That's me,' she said. And then I moved to John 3, and was able to move right on to John 3:16: 'For God so loved the world....'

"It was a wonderful opportunity to share the Good News of the forgiveness of sins in Jesus Christ. My selfish temptation had been to just spend time by myself. But my Lord had a wonderful opportunity to witness to the Gospel *all set up for me!*"

It's not always "talking about Jesus at the water cooler" or slipping tracts or prayer booklets under a *Playboy* magazine in someone's home. But we *are* to "always be prepared to give an answer to everyone who asks you to give the reason for the hope that (we) have" (1 Peter 3:15 NIV).

We are *all* "missionaries."

Your Freudian Slip Is Showing

Mark 16:8 "And they said nothing to any one, for they were afraid"
Theme: Witnessing

As the minister entered the church early one Sunday morning, he was met by a trustee.

"When I came to unlock the church, Pastor," the trustee said in a serious tone, "I found the front door wide open."

"Oh?" replied the pastor. "Did you find anything damaged or missing?"

"Nah," said the trustee. "I looked all over the church and found no signs of evangelism anywhere."

George Murdaugh

SEASONS OF
LENT & EASTER

Lent

Lent is a penitential season beginning with Ash Wednesday and continuing through Holy Week. But as P. H. D. Lang notes in *Ceremony and Celebration:*

> the forty fast days of Lent...do not include the Sundays. The six Sundays within the season of Lent are not fast days but feast days; they are not *of* Lent but *in* Lent. These Sundays, plus Ash Wednesday and the days of Holy Week, are all privileged. No other feast whatsoever is celebrated on them (163).

Accordingly, midweek Lenten services focus on our blessed Lord's passion. Preaching and teaching on the Sundays *in* (not *of*) Lent retain awareness of the season ("Christ our Passover is sacrificed for us"), but Easter is approaching. And Easter is not the *end* of Lent but the *goal* of it. Not only the coming Calvary is ahead of our eyes but also the empty tomb.

Whatever sermon series the preacher chooses for the Sundays in Lent, therefore, the sermons should reflect the Christians' walk as an existential sharing in Christ's death *and* resurrection, as a genuine conformation of their lives to his passion *and* rising again. "We must always speak of the Passion in relation to the Resurrection; we must always speak of sin in relation to grace and the power of Christ's sacrifice" (Nes 117). The same concern, of course, is true in the selection

of hymns. The hymn "Go to Dark Gethsemane" is inappropriate on a Sunday in Lent.

"Is Your Name Paco?"

Luke 15:24 "He was lost and is found!"
Theme: Forgiveness

In Spain, a father and his teenage son were at odds. The relationship became so strained that the son ran away from home. His father, though, began a cross-country journey in search of his rebellious son. Finally, in Madrid, in a last, desperate attempt to find him, his father put an ad in the newspaper: "Dear Paco, meet me in front of the newspaper office at noon. All is forgiven. I love you. Your father."

The next day at noon in front of the newspaper office eight hundred Pacos showed up. They were all seeking forgiveness and love from their fathers.

Is your name Paco?

Often you and I have been rebellious teenage sons or daughters, rebellious older prodigals running away from God's love even here in his house. But our rebellion does not stop our Father, because it is his nature to seek and to save lost people. Here he is still, sending this personal classified ad in Isaiah 53:10 under the headline:

AT-ONE-ment

Jesus, our guilt offering, made us at one with God! Like rebellious teenagers we have been grappling with God. We've been grappling with God, using our pain as a reason for running away from home.

Let me do something which only one of Jesus' shepherds could presume to do: hold a mirror to personal pains which each of us knows intimately. I am going to follow Isaiah's words to talk personally about "soul suffering." It doesn't come through in our English translation, but Isaiah writes about Jesus in our text, "When his soul will have brought a guilt offering" and then follows up in the verse after our text by prophesying about "the suffering of his soul."

Every pang or suffering which we experience is "soul suffering." When we scrape a knee during recess or when the dentist is drilling without anesthetic we suffer. It's not just our knees or our mouths (as if our bodies were vulnerable but our souls untouchable!)—it's *we* who need to hear Jesus saying: "Dear Paco, meet me in my Word. I know the pain of your soul, for I have suffered body and soul for you.

"I know your desperate loneliness, for I was forsaken by my Father for you. I know you, Paco, for I had you in my heart when I gave up my spirit on the cross and I am watching over you with these eyes which opened again in Joseph's tomb. All is forgiven, for I am your guilt offering. I have made atonement for your sin and I love you."

Gregory P. Schulz

The Three-Year-Old Theologian

Romans 7:19 "The evil I do not want is what I do"

Theme: Forgiveness

I remember one Sunday morning, when my son was three years old, I had to pull him out of the morning worship service because he was misbehaving. Often when his mother or I would tell him to do one thing he would do just the opposite. So after a few minutes of this, I grabbed my son and took him into a Sunday school room to administer a little "Law" so that the Gospel could be heard in the service.

Wanting to give him a chance to speak for himself, and wanting to make it perfectly clear as to the reason and purpose for our withdrawal from the service, I asked my son, "Why are you behaving like this? Why are you doing what we tell you *not* to do?"

Naturally, I was expecting my son to lift and drop his shoulders and then say, "I don't know."

But much to my surprise Rieve responded, "Daddy, I don't want to do bad, but I do. I want to do good, but I don't."

His answer surprised me, not simply because he had managed to put together an impressive and complicated sentence structure, balancing his positives and negatives, but because he had in this moment of fear and repentance stated a profound Christian truth. His answer gave me more than what I bargained for. He put into his own words what Paul wrote in Romans 7:18-19.

Just in case you are wondering what happened to Rieve that Sunday morning, I couldn't bring myself to spank such an outstanding theologian after he had made such a profound theological statement of repentance.

So I responded, "Yes, son, you are right. Now let's go back and hear that Jesus forgives all our sins."

Craig Stanford

Getting Caught

2 Samuel 12:7 Nathan said to David, "You are the man!"
Theme: Guilt

In an episode on *Columbo,* Peter Falk visits a woman who has been sleeping with one of her husband's staff.

He quietly asks how some of her husband's crystal goblets got into her lover's apartment. Her husband is a four-star general, and the glasses have four stars on them. She protests that they were a gift to the man.

Now she becomes defiant. She is insulted. She will not *listen* to such filthy accusations. Columbo is quiet, just looking at her.

The woman begins to leave the room. Brazenly she says: "You know the way out!"

Columbo shuffles, and just before she leaves, he says: "Oh, there's just one more question." Slowly he draws a small portable toothbrush out of the pocket of his battered raincoat. It is shaped like a lipstick holder and Columbo found it in the other man's medicine cabinet. Instantly the woman recognizes it as hers.

Her bravado is gone. Her shoulders say. She sighs. The charade is over.

Guilt. Getting *caught.* Have you ever had a similar experience?

The Guilt-Filled Actor

Romans 5:12 "So death spread to all"
Theme: Guilt

The famous British actor, Sir Laurence Olivier, once said, "The worst part of me—the most boring part—is my guilt complex. I feel almost responsible for the fall of Adam and Eve....Once you have those feelings, they don't go away. It [his wife's illness] was my fault, of course. Everything is. What isn't? Now that I've admitted it, I'm looking for a little absolution."

Adapted from *People,* January 10, 1983.

Guilty! Guilty! Guilty!

Ephesians 4:28 "Thieves must give up stealing"
Theme: Guilt

Several bored high school students were driving around one night, trying to find something to do. Finally they came across a construction site. There they saw a sign with a blinking yellow light.

Quickly they put it into their car, and with squeals of delight sped from the scene. Then they tried to turn off the light, but to no avail. The bright yellow beam kept flashing, flashing, flashing. Again and again they tried to extinguish the light, but they could not.

Soon they feared that a police car might see them. And so eventually they returned to the construction site and got rid of the sign.

"I felt that wherever we went with that blinking light, it kept saying to me, '*Guilty! Guilty! Guilty!*'"

Daniel C. Praeuner

No "Once and for All" Repentance

Isaiah 58:2 "Yet day after day they seek me"
Theme: Repentance

A bumper sticker read:

Repent!

Smaller letters underneath noted: "If you have already repented, please disregard this notice."

The Bad Egg

Matthew 15:19 "Out of the heart come evil intentions"
Theme: Sin

There was a five-year-old one time who was happy to receive an Easter basket full of candy, eggs, and toys. That Easter basket was opened and in a matter of days all the candy was eaten, most of the Easter eggs were eaten, and three weeks later, the toys were either broken or lost.

Well, it was six months later and this little five-year-old one day got ready to go to church. In a hurry grabbing his little suit coat, this little one ran out of his room and accidentally dropped his little coat. So he picked it up and rushed to the kitchen, and his mother said to his father, "Do you smell something?" And the little one put his hand into his pocket after he had put on his jacket, and said, "Look, Mom, I found an Easter egg."

I suppose you can imagine the smell, and they needed to be to church in fifteen minutes. That little lad started to cry because he knew that his parents would be angry at him for making them late for church.

We are often like that Easter egg. We look beautiful on the outside, but if someone were to crack us open to see into our hearts, they would more than likely find stinking, six-month-old eggs. Well, that little lad happened to be me. Yes, I did feel bad, but the mess was cleaned up, and my mom and dad *did* forgive me, and we were not late for church after all. My parents were forgiving to me.

God is not angry at us. God is forgiving to us too. God sent his son Jesus to die for our sin. You are forgiven! Christ has cleaned us up. He took on our foulness, our sin, so that we can look good not only on the outside but on the inside as well when we appear before him in his kingdom. God will look at us and say, You good and faithful servant, enter into your master's joy!

Roger T. Blesi

"I Can't Pull That Out!"

James 1:15 "That sin, when it is fully grown, gives birth to death"
Theme: Sin

A boy went for a walk with his grandfather down the gravel road of the farm. He needed to talk. He told his grandfather about all the temptations at school. About the kids who were offering him drugs. About the pressure to go get drunk after school and get in fights. About the fact that his classmates were having sex and how "everybody was doing it." As the boy rattled on and on about his problems the grandfather simply listened as they walked. Finally, the boy finished and they walked on for some time in silence. It was then that the grandfather told the boy to uproot a little weed that was growing along the road. The boy obeyed and pulled out the weed, roots and all. As they walked a little further the grandfather told the boy to pull out, roots and all, a larger plant that was growing along the road. The boy obeyed and pulled out the plant, roots and all, but it was a little more difficult this time. Then as they walked a little further down the road they came to a small tree. The grandfather told the boy to pull it out. This time the boy pulled and pulled until finally it came out, roots and all. Then the grandfather pointed to a full-grown ash tree and repeated the command. The boy looked at his grandfather and laughed, "I can't pull that out!" "Then remember," said the grandfather, "the longer you let sin exist in your life, the harder it is to get rid of it."

How long have you been allowing that sin to grow in you? Today, Christ is calling you to repent and *let go!* You see, he's already paid the price for your sin! You may think that you have strayed too far. You may think that there is no way that you could ever be forgiven for what you've done…and that's exactly what Satan wants you to think!

The truth is, as Christ tells us, "My grace is sufficient for you, for my power is made perfect in weakness." Christ has taken care of it all! He took your sin to the cross and paid the penalty that you deserved—the penalty of death. He loves you enough to willingly lay down his life for you, even when you are against him.

Marc Schwichtenberg

That Screaming Baby

Matthew 15:19 "Out of the heart come evil intentions"
Theme: Sin

A pastor was lying in bed in the middle of the night. His newborn daughter began wailing in the next room. He expected his wife to feed the child, but she quietly reminded him she had done so every night since she had come home from the hospital.

Reluctantly, the pastor got up to share in the wee-hour ritual. He warmed the bottle, fed the baby, got a burp out of her, and, after quietly replacing her in her crib, stumbled back to bed.

Just as he closed his eyes, the baby gave a loud scream. Anger and rage welled up within him. He stalked to her room, but then caught himself. He suddenly realized that in his mind he was actually so angry he was ready to strike the child. He was on the brink of a complete loss of control.

Don Matzat concludes:

> Thus began an eye-opening process of self-knowledge. After numerous other less-dramatic experiences, I came to the conclusion that given the right set of circumstances, I was capable of anything. I was convinced that there was no sin that I could not commit, no perverse act in which I could not participate if the conditions were right. I was afraid of myself. I no longer

admired those who came to Jesus out of great despair
and guilt—I knew that "but for the grace of God, there
go I." For the very first time in my life, I saw myself as
God saw me: wretched, pitiful, poor, blind, and naked. I
really needed Jesus! (39-41).

"You're Blackmailing God!"

Mark 1:40 "If you choose, you can make me clean"
Theme: Suffering

Joni Eareckson became a quadriplegic as the result of a
diving accident at the age of seventeen. A well-meaning friend
tried to convince her it was "God's will" for her to be healed.
But another friend remonstrated with her: "Joni, this whole
thing is getting out of hand. You're twisting God's arm—black-
mailing him."

Joni replied: "Diana, I'm surprised that you'd say that. I
thought you'd have more faith than that."

However, after many healing services it became obvious to
Joni that she wasn't going to be healed. And she gradually
came to a more mature faith...

The wife of a pastor in Fort Wayne was struck by a serious
and debilitating illness. A hospital employee suggested to her
that she wasn't getting better because her faith was inadequate.
Her faith didn't "measure up." "If you had more faith, you
could walk right out of this hospital!"

Later, she writes, she unburdened her confused feelings to
her husband. He reminded her that God is in control and it
isn't our place to tell him what to do. We don't make demands
on our Heavenly Father. Rather we approach his throne with
humility, adding the words, "If it be thy will."

We trust him with the outcome.

Greg Lockwood

Easter

In "Easter: A Time for Renewal of Hope," (Aho et al. 77), Richard Kapfer suggests that on Easter morning, instead of having a sanctuary filled with lilies and Easter banners, let the sanctuary be as barren of color as it was on Good Friday. Let the cross still be veiled, lights be dimmed, and any organ music be somber in tone.

This more accurately recalls the first Easter morning, which began with gloom and hopelessness. He suggests that we begin with the women at the tomb and that Psalm 130 be explored. First we are to repent and wait and hope (Aho et al. 77-81.) Only then do we hear the proclamation from the empty tomb: "He is not here! He is risen!"

Kapfer continues:

> Only at this point can the lights come on, the banners be
> lifted, the cross unveiled, and the trumpets sound forth.
> Now the congregation is ready to respond to an
> announcement "JESUS CHRIST IS RISEN TODAY!" with the
> words "HE IS RISEN INDEED!" (81).

He concludes his sermon:

> Now let the lights come on in your life; and live in the
> light! Now let the cross be unveiled, for it is a glorious
> cross of forgiveness! Now let the banners be raised in

your life of faith! Now let the lilies of joy trumpet their praise to God: He is risen! Hallelujah! Hope is renewed forever and ever! (82).

The alternative, of course, is the historic Easter Vigil, wherein

we have the modern adaptation of the ancient Night Watch in which the faithful would gather in the churches in the night of Easter awaiting that hour toward sunrise when Christ arose from the tomb ("The Easter Vigil" *Una Sancta* 14, no. 2 (1957): 5 [see also vol. 20, no. 2 (1963)], quoted in Lang 169-170.)

The illustrations for Easter and its season echo this tone of triumph and victory.

Preparing Your Own Funeral Service

1 Corinthians 15:22 "So all will be made alive in Christ"
Theme: Easter

Staring Death in the Face

It was a chilly early November day as I walked up the steps and rang Ed's doorbell. The yard had just been raked by his grandsons, and its neat appearance was matched by a clean living room that was the pride of the man sitting in the lounge chair. Although he was very ill with an advancing cancer, he could still take care of his surroundings.

Ed was more agitated than usual. There was something on his mind, but he couldn't bring himself to talk about it until I offered to share Holy Communion with him, signaling that my visit would soon be over. Suddenly he rose from his chair with an unaccustomed swiftness and disappeared into the bedroom, soon to emerge with a sheet of notepaper in his hand.

"Tell me, Pastor, what do you think of a woman who would do this?" As I unfolded the paper, I read the outline of a funeral service written in a very neat hand by Ed's wife, Edna, who had died three years before.

"I think that's wonderful, Ed," I answered. "What a witness she gave to you and your family by asking for certain hymns and readings!" Then the Holy Spirit turned on the lightbulb for me. "Ed," I asked softly, "do you want to do something like this?"

"Yes," came the reply, almost more of a sigh than a word. We spent the next hour talking about his funeral and making notes together. Then we shared the sacrament and Ed was at peace...

Renewal Celebrated

About ten weeks later, in middle January, I received a call to come to Ed's bedside. We prayed and cried and sang together. Two days later we celebrated his victory won by Christ with the liturgy he had helped to write. At the head of his casket was the paschal candle like the one we lighted this morning at an early hour. On that November afternoon Ed had said, "I'm not a great candle man, Pastor, but if it will say that Christ is alive and has me in his hands, go ahead." We did, and Christ is alive, and we live in him. We celebrate the death of death in all its manifestations, including the brokenness of sin in our lives, for Christ is risen!

Donald W. Sandmann

The New "I"

Galatians 2:20 "It is no longer I who live"
Theme: Easter

Because Christ was raised from the dead, we now walk in newness of life (Rom 6:4).

In his youth, St. Augustine was a profligate. However, through the prayers of his sainted mother, Monica, he was converted and he became one of the great fathers of the church.

One day in his later life he was walking through a part of town he had frequented in his younger days. A woman recognized him, and called out to him: "Augustine! Augustine!"

Augustine ignored the call, so the woman cried out again: "Augustine! Augustine! It is I!"

But Augustine, turning neither to the right nor the left, kept walking straight ahead, saying: "But it is not 'I'!"

The old "I" had now died to sin. And the "chief character" in his life now was the resurrected Christ, the "Christ within" into whose name he had been baptized.

"Tell Me Fifty Times a Day!"

Luke 24:38 "Why do doubts arise in your hearts?"
Theme: Resurrection

"But I just told you that yesterday!" the college student told his girlfriend. He didn't understand why she needed to hear those three magic words over and over again. Was she insecure? Was she afraid they weren't true? Why did she need this constant reassurance? The girlfriend explained why in unforgettable words: "Honey, you have to tell me you love me fifty times a day or I'll forget!" (Husbands, take note!)

That's a true story. And the point this young lady makes is very important: we need the constant reassurance of those things that are most important to us. Just hearing it one time isn't enough; we need it over and over again.

In the Lukan Gospel, the disciples have already heard reports that Jesus is risen—but one report isn't enough! They need Jesus to personally come and prove that he has risen to conquer their fears. And he did!

We too often have fears and doubts. But the resurrected Christ assures us: "Peace be with you!" and he comes to us again and again in Word and sacrament assuring us! "I am with you always, to the very end of the age" (Mt 28:20 NIV).

Brian J. Hamer

"On the Other Side"

John 11:25 "Those who believe in me,
even though they die, will live"
Theme: Resurrection

A young teenage girl had been severely ill for over a year. Her last days on earth were marked by several operations, months of hospitalization, and a full $1 million of medical care. Death was imminent. It was Jesus' promise of our resurrection that allowed her uncle, a pastor, to lean into her ear and whisper the last words she heard on earth: "I'll see you on the other side."

These two Christians knew Jesus' promise to someday halt the great funeral procession of the world and announce with a trumpet the time for all Christians to arise, to meet him in the air, and to gather around his throne in eternal worship.

Brian J. Hamer

ORDINARY TIME
(SEASON AFTER
PENTECOST)

ORDINARY TIME (SEASON AFTER PENTECOST)

First of all, let us dispel the myth that Pentecost is "the birthday of the church." Acts 2:42 says the Lord "*added* to their number" (NIV). The "church" was in existence *before* Pentecost. There already was an *ekklesia* which believed in the resurrection (including the first one to believe: our blessed Lord's mother did not go out to the tomb with the other women *because she knew he was not there*).

Second, Pentecost should be "celebrated with great festivity and rejoicing over the outpouring of the Holy Spirit" (Lang 171).

Would that our people might observe it with the same fervor as they do Christmas and Easter! When a survey was made in one congregation, seventy-eight percent of the members could not think of a single thing to say about Pentecost. Have you ever heard someone say, "Are you ready for Pentecost?"

This is not to promote a "Have a Peppy Pentecost" approach. But we do need to emphasize more the oldest of the three great festivals of the church year. (Its roots are in the Hebrew Scriptures when Israel celebrated the "feast of the weeks" fifty days after the first fruits of the harvest had been gathered.)

A parish might have a Parade of Nations or read the lessons or Apostle's Creed in various languages, representing the diversity of ethnic traditions within the congregation.

Special prayers could call for the increased indwelling of the Holy Spirit. This is the powerful, blessed Holy Spirit who

- Christ promised would come to us (Jn 15:26);

- calls us by the Gospel and keeps us in the one true faith;

- "will teach [us] all things, and bring to [our] remembrance all that I have said to you" (Jn 14:26);

- will be with us through all of life's trials, putting the very words into our mouths to say to our accusers (Mt 10:19);

- "produces love, joy, peace, patience, kindness, goodness, faithfulness, humility and self-control" (Gal 5:22-23a TEV).

It is all these "fruits of the Spirit" (Gal 5 and 6) to which the Christian is called and to which the following illustrations are directed in the Season after Pentecost.

The beauty of observing the church year is that we see the whole of our Lord's life—and the life to which the Christian is called—spelled out dramatically as the pericopal lessons pass before our eyes.

The walk of the Christian is seen in its many facets in the Season after Pentecost. The illustrations which follow cover a variety of dimensions in Christian living and focus on the marks of being a Christian in the world.

But it should be noted that one doesn't "work on" emulating Christian virtues. That is the evil of moralism, which exalts a value as a way one achieves spirituality. Biblical Christianity sees any virtue as the result of the Gospel active in the believer's life.

Further, Christ is not just "guide," "model," or "example." He is rather "prototype." We focus not on his humility as a precept to follow but on his humiliation—his sacrifice for us. For we fail totally. But through his death and resurrection, we are forgiven and then called to the fruits of faith, empowered solely by the Holy Spirit (see Gal 5 and 6). Christ as prototype is the first fruits of those who believe in him. It is "Christ in me" (see Col 1:27).

These illustrations are also an implicit challenge to those who are living primarily for the "now" to examine what they are living for, how they are living, and how they will die. For we are all terminal.

But my serious note at times (for example, with illustrations dealing with death at the end of the Season after Pentecost) is not to leave one with a doomsday mentality but rather to focus on what is truly important in life. There is great need for a positive, "turned out" approach in our Christian walk. The Holy Spirit calls us to evidence the "power to be" little Christs, new persons reaching out, helping others, boldly sharing Christ.

But at the same time, as Thomas à Kempis said in his classic, *The Imitation of Christ,* we are to be "turned in" to the interior life. So the following illustrations are intended to direct readers to more spiritual introspection—and to Christ in whom alone true peace and joy are found.

The Smelly Old Bag Lady

John 15:12 "Love one another"
Theme: Acceptance

There is an old woman who was once a bag lady in Detroit. Alcohol had gotten the best of her, and the alcohol most likely was the reason she was homeless. To honestly describe her, she was a disgusting, drunken, foul-mouthed, mean, old bum.

You would never invite her to your home because she was very rude and her body smelled.

One evening before Thanksgiving a relative of hers got a call from the police. They wanted to know if this old lady was related to this family. It was a surprise to find this long-lost aunt. Because she never had spoken with the family, they assumed that she had died long ago.

The family went and got the homeless lady and invited her into their home and asked her to Thanksgiving dinner the next day.

On Thanksgiving Day, as the prayer was being said, the old lady began to sob uncontrollably. Finally, when she could talk, she explained that she was so happy, and that if she had known that they had still loved her, she wouldn't have lived on the streets for the last twelve years. This is a true story. *I was present at the table that day.*

What about you? Have you been living apart from God's love, when it has always been there for you, because you can't imagine that God loves you the way you are?

Be assured that God loves you always—completely—and is waiting to welcome you home right now.

Cory Fanning

The Lazy Lover

James 2:26 "Faith without works...is dead"
Theme: Action

A man wrote to a young woman for months until she finally agreed to meet with him. "Come to such and such a place, at such and such an hour," she said to him.

At that time and place the lover finally found himself seated beside his beloved. He then reached into his pocket and pulled out a sheaf of love letters that he had written to her. They were passionate letters, expressing the pain he felt and his burning desire to experience the delights of love and union. He began to read them to her. But he just continued to read on and on.

Finally the woman said, "What kind of a fool are you? These letters are all about me and your longing for me. Well, here I am sitting with you at last   and you are lost in your stupid letters. Why don't you *do* something about it!"

Adapted from Anthony DeMello, 101

A Piece of Dead Wood

1 Peter 3:21 "Baptism...now saves you"
Theme: Baptism

Have you ever seen two trees or bushes growing so close together that you can't distinguish which fruit belongs to which tree? That is the way it is now with us and Christ. God is pleased with our fruit because our limbs have intermingled with the tree of Christ. Our lives, our limbs, are so intertwined with Christ that our fruit is Christ's fruit, and Christ's fruit is our fruit.

Baptism is how it all got started. Jesus' life and death were applied to you when you were still a dead piece of wood which the pastor was holding over the baptismal font. But

God's Word and the water changed all that. In a split second, in the blink of an eye, while angels watched you and the sanctuary was filled with the sound of their wings, God made you alive. He changed you from a dead piece of wood to a live young tree. God spoke the words "You are mine" as the pastor said "I baptize you," and heaven applauded, for once more the life of God became the life of a child. Once more death was swallowed up in victory. Once more hell wept and heaven rejoiced because you were made one with your Father through the blood of Jesus Christ. That's what happened in your baptism.

And every Sunday as we partake of Christ's body and blood our baptismal relationship with our Heavenly Father is strengthened as our sins are wiped away and God reassures us of his love. As we taste the wine and the bread, we remember that Christ tasted of death once and for all for us. We remember that he took the ax for us.

Chad Bird

"The Touch of Your Hand"

Galatians 6:2 "Bear one another's burdens"
Theme: Caring

Last week I met a woman up by the parish house and I was kidding with her. I said, "What are you doing up here?" She said, "I've come to see Sister Pat for a massage." Sister Pat Reynolds does healing and touch massage and teaches others how to do it. So, I kidded, "A massage, huh?" And suddenly she turned serious and said something that hit me in the gut. She said softly, "I live alone, and no one ever touches me."

William J. Bausch, *More Telling Stories*, 4

Hell's Angels in the Church

**Psalm 122:1 "I was glad when they said to me,
"'Let us go to the house of the LORD!'"**
Theme: Church

There is a church in Concord, California, where a group of forty Hell's Angels roared up into the parking lot just before the service was to begin. One Hell's Angel got off his bike, walked into the church, and sat down. The whole congregation watched fearfully, wondering what would happen next. But the rest of the bikers just stood in the parking lot and smoked their cigarettes during the hour, waiting for the service to end.

When it was over, some members talked to the bikers and invited the group to stay for coffee, which they did. Then they learned why the one biker had come to the service. He in some way had broken their "code" and as punishment had to go to church.

Perhaps going to church is a "punishment" for some people. And even for faithful Christians, at times it may be a "painful" experience if the service is   poorly planned or the sermon isn't too inspiring that day. More than once we may wince when we sing the lines in the hymn:

> Grant us courage
> For the facing of this hour

But the faithful concentration on God's Word can make all the difference. We need to train ourselves to constantly ask: "Lord, what would you teach me here?" What word do you have for me today?"

> Let the words of my mouth and the meditation
>   of my heart
> be acceptable in thy sight,
> O LORD, my rock and my redeemer" (Ps 19:14).

"You Have No Right to Be Here!"

Mark 12:30 "You shall love the Lord your God with all your heart"
Theme: Commitment

It was Sunday morning in South America, in a little chapel on the border of Venezuela and Colombia. As the worship service was beginning, a not uncommon occurrence happened: a band of guerrillas armed with machine guns came out of the jungle and crashed and banged their way into the chapel. The pastor and the congregation were totally horrified and afraid. They dragged the pastor outside to be executed. Then the leader of the guerrillas came back into the chapel and demanded, "Anyone else who believes in this God stuff, come forward!" Everyone was petrified. They stood frozen. There was a long silence.

Finally, one man came forward and stood in front of the guerrilla chief and said simply, "I love Jesus." And he was roughly tossed to the soldiers and also taken out to be executed. And several other Christians came forward saying the same thing and they too were driven outside. Then the sound of machine gun fire. When there were no more people left willing to identify themselves as Christians, the guerrilla chief returned inside and told the remaining congregation to get out. "You have no right to be here." And with that he herded them out of the chapel where they were astonished to see their pastor and those others standing there.

The pastor and those people were ordered to go back into the chapel to continue the service while the others were angrily warned to stay out "until," said the guerrilla chief, "you have the courage to stand up for your beliefs!" And with that the guerrillas disappeared into the jungle (adapted from William J. Bausch, *More Telling Stories*, 13-14).

"A Right to Be Here?"

And you—here this morning—do you have "a right to be here"? Do you believe in this stuff? I mean, really believe? By the power of the Holy Spirit, are you totally committed to Christ? And by his power alone, are you honestly living that way and making choices and leaps of faith that way when decision time comes?

Otherwise, "you have no right to be here."

You and I are to live and die for Christ...to be faithful unto death, in the sure and certain hope of the resurrection from the dead...born to be with God forever.

But the question is: are you and I always living that way...today?

Mark 12:30 (NIV) says: "You must love the Lord your God with all your heart, and with all your soul, and with all your mind, and with all your strength." The point is: *Although we are* curvatus in se, *curved in on ourselves, and often make only partial* commitment to our Lord, he calls us to die to self and give our *total* dedication to him....

Do you have "a right to be here"? *You most certainly do!* For you are baptized—in grace! As the pastor says in a Slovak communion service, just before giving the penitents the body and blood of our Lord (and he places his hands on the head of each person kneeling before him):

> "Rejoice, child of God, because your sins *have been forgiven* through the precious, shed blood of our Lord and Savior Jesus Christ!"

Thanks be to God!

> I kneel before thee, Jesus, crucified,
> My cross is shouldered and my self denied;
> I'll follow daily, closely—will not flee
> To lose myself, for love of man and Thee. Amen
> (J. R. W. Stott, *Basic Christianity* [Leicester, United Kingdom: Inter-Varsity Press, 1970], 121).

Garbage!

2 Timothy 1:13 (KJV) "Hold fast the form of sound words"
Theme: Communication

A harried couple worked at different hours. Often they saw each other only briefly on a given day.

So they took to leaving messages on a blackboard on their refrigerator. They were words of affection but also reminders of chores to be done or appointments to be kept, and so on.

One morning the husband appeared at the breakfast table looking terribly hurt.

"What's wrong honey? You look upset!" asked the wife.

"I don't think you read my message," said her husband, pouting.

She rushed to the refrigerator and there read the words:

I Love You

Garbage

Timothy Sims

Shoot the Lepers!

Luke 17:12 "Ten lepers approached him"
Theme: Communication

While teaching my Sunday school class recently, I noticed some wide-eyed looks of amazement as we discussed our lesson, Luke 17:12-19. Encouraged with their enthusiasm, I asked how they would feel if, like Jesus, they were entering a town on foot and were met by ten lepers.

"I'd be scared to death, but I'd probably shoot them," answered one of my first grade boys.

"Beau!" I said, horrified, "do you know what a leper is?"

"Of course," came the confident reply. "It's one of those big yellow cats with black spots all over him."

Suzanne Swartz Kirklin

"Did You Hear a Coin Drop?"

1 Samuel 3:9-10 "Speak, LORD, for your servant is listening"
Theme: Communication

Two men were walking along a crowded city sidewalk. Suddenly one of them remarked, "Listen to the lovely sound of that cricket." The friend walking alongside of him could not hear the sound. He asked his companion how he could detect the sound of a cricket amid the roar of the traffic and the cacophony of voices, footsteps, horns, and the like. The first man, having been raised on a farm, had trained himself to hear the sounds of nature—but he didn't have to explain. He simply pulled a quarter from his pocket, dropped it on the sidewalk, and a dozen nearby people looked down to the sidewalk to search for the coin's whereabouts. He said, "We hear what we listen for."

Isn't the same true for you and me? There are so many voices vying for our attention that the voice of God, calling out our name, is lost in a sea of other voices demanding equal time and attention. We need to focus our attention, to be alert to the voice of God. We hear what we listen for.

Jeff A. J. Maissan

"Gladly, the Cross-Eyed Bear"

2 Timothy 1:13 (KJV) "Hold fast the form of sound words"
Theme: Communication

Clear communication is very important. Here are some misunderstood Biblical phrases:

- "The Lord is my shepherd; I've got all I want."

- There's the boy who likes tennis and hears about the time "Moses served in Pharaoh's court."

- There's the child impressed by the shortest man in the Bible: "Knee-high-Miah" or David, "the Shoe-High-Mite."

- There's the baseball fan who perked up when the lesson began "In the Big Inning."

- There's the physician's son who couldn't understand why Moses took two tablets of *stone*.

- "Many are called but few are frozen."

- "Eat carrots for me." ("He careth for me.")

- "Gladly, the cross-eyed bear."

- And then there were children at an Army post chapel singing: "Praise him, Praise him, Army little children!"

"Marriage Is Holy Acrimony"

2 Timothy 1:13 (KJV) "Hold fast the form of sound words"
Theme: Communication

According to a Chevy Chase church newsletter, children said the following during confirmation classes there:

- Noah's wife was Joan of Ark.

- The Fourth Commandment is "humor thy father and mother."

- When Mary heard she was to be the mother of Jesus, she went off and sang the Magna Carta.

- Another name for marriage is holy acrimony.

- Christians have only one wife—that's called monotony.

- The patron saint of travelers is St. Francis of Seasick.

- The natives of Macedonia did not believe, so Paul got stoned.

- The First Commandment was when Eve told Adam to eat the apple.

- It is sometimes difficult to hear in church because the agnostics are so terrible.

That Strange Bouquet

2 Timothy 1:13 (KJV) "Hold fast the form of sound words"
Theme: Communication

A legal firm sent a large bouquet of flowers to a branch office that was having a grand opening in Baltimore.

When the officials arrived from New York to celebrate the day they saw these words over the flowers which they had sent:

Our Sincere Sympathy

Immediately they phoned the florist and asked him what had happened.

"Good heavens!" the florist responded with a gasp. "That means the flowers I sent to the funeral home read:

Congratulations on
Your New Location

"I'm an Atheist"

Isaiah 55:6 "Seek the LORD while he may be found"
John 10:10 "I came that they may have life"
Theme: Doubt

A young woman walked into a pastor's office and announced, "I'm an atheist." To which the pastor replied, "Well, tell me what kind of a God you don't believe in." And she told him—for an hour. And when the hour was over, the pastor said, "You know, I think I must be an atheist, too. Because I don't believe in that God either!"

And then he told her of the God he believed in—a loving, forgiving, contemporary, and discoverable God who will come to us when we but seek him in his Word and sacraments.

And even then, when we have used the means of grace and don't have a clear answer, when we are saying, "Where are you, God? Why, God?" God is saying to us as a knowing, loving Father, "My child, at this point it is still not for you to know. Trust me. I know the thoughts that I think toward you, thoughts of peace and not of evil." Again: "Mine hour is not yet come."

Then we may have to say with Paul: "O the depth of the riches both of the wisdom and knowledge of God! How unsearchable are his judgments, and his ways past finding out! (Rom 11:33 KJV).

Donald L. Deffner, *Best of Your Life,* 85-86

Eating Sour Grapes

Ezekiel 18:2 "The parents have eaten sour grapes,
and the children's teeth are set on edge"
Theme: Eucharist

When I was young I would go to my grandmother's house and eat the grapes growing in her back yard. Of course, most of the time they were not ripe and very sour. I could never seem to figure out that they were good to eat only in the fall, and so all summer I would try every time I was there to see if they were ripe yet and they usually weren't. And every time I would have to go into the house with my teeth on edge, sit down at the kitchen table, and ask my grandma to help me get rid of the taste. Her answer to my trouble was always the same. She would give me a glass of grape juice. It was sweet and took care of the problem without conflicting with the sour grape taste. It just obliterated it and tasted good as well.

Our Heavenly Father has the same cure. When we have been eating sour grapes and want to be forgiven he invites us to his table where the sweet wine of the Eucharist has become the blood of Jesus Christ and the bread of the altar is the Body of our Lord. The sour is obliterated and we are refreshed and renewed. The sour grapes of our sin are turned into the sweet blessing of the sacrament of the altar in the person of Jesus Christ. And so we are freed from the bitterness of sin without hope for forgiveness. We are new creations.

Charles Varsogea

In the Vicelike Grip of Fear

1 Peter 5:7 "Cast all your anxiety on him"
Theme: Faith

A minister tells of a woman, a happy and efficient wife of a fellow pastor, who was experiencing her full share of life's sunshine and shade, with no real darkness falling her way. Then, without warning, her husband died of a heart attack, leaving her terribly alone and afraid—afraid of her own decisions, afraid of the present, afraid of the future.

When the minister visited his colleague's wife, he found her in the vicelike grip of fear—so tyrannized that most of her time was spent in bed. She was so terrified that she had become bedridden.

When the minister saw her two years later, he was pleasantly surprised to find a poised, serene woman working as a receptionist in an insurance office. When the pastor asked her to explain her amazing recovery, the woman replied, "The work helped, of course, but I couldn't work at all until I faced my fear and saw it was basically a selfish rebellion against God and what I thought was God's will. When I saw that, I began to pray that God would forgive my selfishness. And as I prayed, I became aware of God's hand reaching down to me, and the Holy Spirit moved me to reach up in faith until I finally clasped that hand. And then to my amazement, I found his hand clasping mine; and I knew that he really cared and that he would help me as long as I held his hand in faith."

Donald L. Deffner, *Sermon Illustrations for the Gospel Lessons*, 25

Faith, Not Sight

2 Corinthians 5:7 "We walk by faith, not by sight"
Theme: Faith

A pastor relates that his mother is near-blind, but that she won't admit it. She just will not confess that she can't see.

One day, as he walked with her from the car to their front door, he said, "Ma, the door's straight ahead." His mother promptly turned to the right and smacked head-on into the wall of the house.

Again the pastor said quietly, "Ma, the door's straight ahead." Again she turned and walked right into the wall.

There was a moment's pause, and then she said, "Teddy, where's the door?"

Time and again we insist on going our own way. Often it is only when we meet with utter failure that we turn to God and plead for his direction and help.

The Scared Preacher

Genesis 26:24 "Do not be afraid, for I am with you"
Theme: Fear

A young seminarian stood in the pulpit for the very first time to deliver his very first sermon. As he stood there, he was shaking. His knees were knocking together. As he began to speak, he began to stutter. He said, "Before I got up here this morning, only God and I knew what I was going to say. And now that I'm up here, only God knows!"

Daniel Olson

Quite Another Story

Ephesians 4:31 "Put away all...wrangling"
Theme: Fellowship

A Sunday school teacher had just concluded a fascinating account of all the joys and wonders of heaven. "Now!" she said, beaming at the class, "How many of you want to go there?"

All of the children's hands shot up, except one. Puzzled, the teacher asked the boy, "Don't you want to go to heaven?!"

The boy just looked around at the class and said: "Yeah, but not with *this* crowd!"

> To live above with the saints we love
> Ah, that must be the highest glory.
> But to live below, with the saints we know,
> Is quite another story! (Old Irish ditty).

The Password

Ephesians 2:8 "For by grace you have been saved"
Theme: Grace, God's

Imagine this scene: A person has just arrived at the portals of heaven. A voice asks: "What is the password? Speak it and you may enter."

"The password?" the person replies tremulously. "Well, is it: 'Whoever calls on the name of the Lord shall be saved'?"

"No," replies the voice.

"'The just shall live by faith'?"

"No."

"'For God so loved the world that he gave...'?"

"No."

"'There is no longer any condemnation to them that are in Christ Jesus'?'

"Those are all true sayings," says the voice, "but they are not the password for which I listen today."

"Well, then, I give up," says the person.

And the voice says, "That's it! Come right in!"

You and I are saved by grace alone! Oh, may God the Holy Spirit move you again to rejoice in the presence of God here this morning.

Donald L. Deffner, "The Wounded Healer Returns to Restore Us," *Concordia Pulpit for 1990*, 76-80

"This Christianity Stuff Really Works!"

John 7:17 "Anyone who resolves to do the will of God will know whether the teaching is from God"
Theme: Grace, Means of

A pastor in Ann Arbor, Michigan, tells of a woman who lived near his church who was well known for her negativity. In fact, she was not only a hostile person, but she fairly "seethed with hate," he said. She had been a church member up until twenty years ago. But something had happened (no one could now remember what) which had so changed her that for, yes, *twenty years,* she was literally filled with loathing.

And yet, somehow, the pastor recounts, the woman happened to visit the church again. She attended services and meetings for about a month. And then one day, to his complete surprise, the woman walked up to him in the church hall and he saw a totally different person. To his amazement the smiling, beaming woman said to him: "Hey, you know, this Christianity stuff *really* works!"

That's all there is to the story. It's a true story. It really happened. It's no more "dramatic" than that.

And yet, it's *quite* "dramatic." "Christianity really works!" The warming fellowship of being with other Christians *really works*. God's means of grace, his holy Word and sacraments, *really work*. God in his merciful forgiveness, by the power of the Holy Spirit, does that within us which we are unable to do. *Christianity really works.*

Coleridge was once asked: "Is Christianity true?" He replied: "Try it."

The Eight-Point Buck

Mark 9:43 "If your hand causes you to stumble, cut it off"
Theme: Hyperbole

Some friends who went deer hunting separated into pairs for the day. And that night one hunter returned alone, staggering under an eight-point buck. "Where's Harry?" asked another hunter. "Oh, he fainted a couple of miles up on the trail," Harry's partner answered. "And you left him lying there all alone and carried the deer back?" "A tough call," said the hunter. "But I figured no one's going to steal Harry."

And that story is cousin to the old exclamation, "If I've told you once, I've told you a million times not to exaggerate!"

It's what we call hyperbole, using extravagant language to get a point across. I introduce the story and mention the use of hyperbole because, as you heard in the Gospel this morning, you were subjected to such outrageous, terrible sounding things as plucking out eyes and cutting off arms in order to get to heaven. But we have to recognize that Jesus is using hyperbole here, severely exaggerated speech to make a point...

William J. Bausch, *More Telling Stories*, 1

"Listen Slowly"

Ephesians 6:4 "Do not provoke your children to anger"
Theme: Listening

I vividly remember some time back being caught in the undertow of too many commitments in too few days. It wasn't long before I was snapping at my wife and our children, choking down my food at mealtimes, and feeling irritated at those unexpected interruptions through the day. Before long, things around our home started reflecting the pattern of my hurry-up style. It was becoming unbearable.

I distinctly recall after supper one evening the words of our younger daughter, Colleen. She wanted to tell me about something important that had happened to her at school that day. She hurriedly began, "Daddy-I-wanna-tell-you-somethin'-and-I'll-tell-you-really-fast."

Suddenly realizing her frustration, I answered, "Honey, you can tell me...and you don't have to tell me really fast. Say it slowly."

I'll never forget her answer: "Then listen slowly."

Adapted from Charles Swindoll, *Stress Fractures*

"Where Is Your Brother?"

Luke 15:20 "His father...was filled with compassion"
Theme: Love, A Father's

When I was seven years old, my brother and I shared a bedroom on the top floor of our three-story house. On the Fourth of July that year there was a storm that flooded our basement and shook our house with thunder. One of those peals of thunder shook a lightbulb in our bedroom closet and woke me up. When I saw the light coming out from under the closet door, I thought it was a fire, so I ran downstairs to tell my father, who was bailing out our basement.

All the way down both flights of stairs I was worried about my brother. When I found my father I told him what I had seen and this is what happened. My father was standing knee deep in water with a bucket in his left hand and a fear of fire that he had had since he was young. He put his right hand on my shoulder and said in a very calm voice, "Where is your brother?"

It was because of those four words that I came to understand what it was to be a brother and that I learned what my father's will really was. Together we ran back up both flights of stairs to check on my brother.

So it is in God's family. It is not the recognition or even confession of the fact that we are less than what we should be that gives us the power to turn our lives around. It is the very real presence of the Father among us and the clear calm declaration of his love for each of us in the person of our Lord and savior Jesus Christ that makes us different. It is, in short, the Gospel.

Charles Varsogea

"We Found a Donor"

Isaiah 49:15 "Can a woman forget her nursing child?"
Theme: Love, Selfless

There was a boy who was born with no ears. Shortly after he was born surgery was performed to enable him to hear.

Later he was told that in time he would be able to have an operation to transplant some ears.

He grew up enduring ridicule throughout grade school and high school. Now he was in college. He would call home frequently to see if a donor had been found. By this time he had been told he was ready for a transplant. But each time he phoned, his father gave him the same response. No donor had been found.

Then one day he received a phone call from his father. A donor *had* been found! So he flew home for the surgery. The operation was successful. And he returned to college, thankful for the blessing God had given him.

Not long after that, he received a phone call from his father. His father said his mother was critically ill, that she might not last through the night.

Immediately the young man left the college and went home. When he arrived at the airport, he could tell from the look on his father's face that his mother had died.

They went directly to the funeral home. As they approached the casket, the father put his arm around his son and said, "You know, son, your mother loved you very much."

"I know, Dad," the son responded.

Then the father reached down into the casket and brushed aside his wife's hair. Her ears were now gone.

Jerrold L. Nichols

Loving the Unlovable

1 John 4:19 "We love because he first loved us"
Theme: Love, Unconditional

How do you bring yourself to love—not simply to agree that it's what you should do, but actually to love *some* people?

I first got to know Bob out in Provo, Utah, because his wife was a member of our congregation. Gladys was one of those whom pastors refer to when they say, "If only I had twenty, no, just ten more like her!" Her Christianity was her loveliness.

Bob, on the other hand, was something else: he was a big, hulking brute of a man: a former bare-knuckles brawler; mean, crude, a threatening presence. There was something about him that repelled you, a look in his eyes that I can only describe as evil.

I didn't think I liked Bob very much.

Gladys started having trouble with her legs: bad circulation and blood clots. Then gangrene set in. Amputations followed—first one leg, then the other.

Did this soften Bob up? Did this make him one who could reach out in gentleness?

Bob confided in me: *he* was the one in a bad way; *he* was the one really suffering because of this. You see, there was no more sex. His wife wasn't a whole woman any more. How can you make love to a freak?

I was sure I didn't like Bob much at all. Love him? Ha! You couldn't even *like* such a man.

Then Gladys died and was mercifully received in heaven by her Lord Jesus. Bob attended the funeral, of course, crying his eyes out in despair, like those who have no hope.

She was taken mercifully, I thought, not so much from a world of pain and suffering, but now she wouldn't have to put up with Bob any longer. And it served him right, I thought, to feel the pain of her absence. He was so dependent on her, yet look how he treated her!

But then a surprising thing happened: Bob started coming to church on Sundays, always sitting in the back and leaving right away.

So I continued my visits. But there was still that threatening presence that created fear, that meanness, that evil gleam in his eyes. There was the twelve-gauge shotgun propped up behind the front door. And there was no perceptible response to God's Word.

Bob remarried quickly, to relieve his great suffering caused by Gladys. She was a retired Mormon woman he met at the senior citizen center. She put an end to my visits.

A month later Bob blew her brains all over their bedroom wall with his .45 gun and then turned the gun on himself and did the other wall.

Yes! I was justified! There was good reason why I didn't like Bob at all. How could you ever *love* something like him?

Those whom Jesus quoted were right! "An eye for an eye..." Bob did the world a favor when he turned the gun on himself, didn't he? We're all better off without him.

Yes, love your neighbor, but *hate* your enemy! Bob was *undeserving* of love.

Do you see what was happening? When it came to Bob, I had become a Pharisee in pastor's clothing!

I had allowed the reactions of natural man to fill my heart with anger, resentment, and revulsion. And it blinded me, making me incapable of loving as Jesus bids me love.

You will have your own "Bobs" in life, and the challenge will be there for you to respond as Jesus bids.

It was this Word of Jesus in Matthew 5 that began to haunt me and drive me to repentance: "Love your enemies, John," Jesus says.

And I was driven to the throne of grace to cry out, "Dear God, forgive my lovelessness, but how, how can I *love* a man like Bob?"

The answer was right there in Jesus' words—and it had been there all along: "Love your enemies....Be perfect, as your heavenly Father is perfect" (Mt 5:44,48).

Jesus directs us here not to the attaining of sinless perfection but to the unconditional love of our heavenly Father.

Here is his perfection: He loves the loveless and the unlovable.

To them he gives the unspeakably priceless gift of his own Son's life.

For the totally undeserving there is forgiveness, sonship, and love.

And the enabling power of Jesus' words for you and for me to accomplish what he bids us do lies in this truth: "totally undeserving, loveless, unlovable" describes *me* and it describes *you!*

The old Pharisee in each of us needs to hear this.

Yes, *I* was Jesus' "Bob"! It was *my* sin that nailed Jesus' hands and feet to that cross.

Ultimately, we are the enemies who are loved; we are those for whom Jesus prays. We are undeserving, yet we so freely receive.

And now, with this love as their motivation, the Father's children love as he loves.

What could possibly move you to love the "Bobs" in your life?

Just this: "We love," says John, "because he first loved us" (1 Jn 4:19).

His love the cause, the source, the enabling power; ours the response.

How can we, the truly undeserving, who have received the unspeakably priceless treasures of God's grace, how can we withhold our love from others and now treat them as we have been so mercifully treated?

Loving others may not always seem reasonable or even easy. But nowhere does Jesus call us to do the reasonable or easy thing! Instead, he calls us to deny ourselves, to take up our cross (our "Bobs"!) and follow him. To follow him in loving them, forgiving them, and lifting them up, all the while basking in the radiance of the shadow of his cross! In the name of him who loves the loveless and the unlovable, who feeds them with the riches of his grace, Amen.

John Stube

The Auto Accident

Ephesians 5:25 "Husbands, love your wives"
Theme: Marriage

There's a story about a man who was finally enjoying his greatest pleasure. He got the car he had wanted all his life. But his wife wanted to drive it. He said, "Well, okay." And so she drove it.

But wouldn't you know, she got into an accident and totaled the car. Can you imagine how she felt!?

She was okay. But you know how it is. She had to fill out an insurance report on the accident. So she reached into the glove compartment of the car to get the forms and the auto registration. And there was an envelope next to the forms.

The lady opened the envelope, and there was a note attached. She could recognize her husband's handwriting. And the note said: "Honey, remember, it's *you* I love, not the car."

Adapted from a story by Paul Harvey, related by Ken Larson

The Unity Candle

Genesis 2:24 "And they become one flesh"
Theme: Marriage

A bride and groom were discussing their upcoming wedding ceremony with the pastor. They were discussing the lighting of the "unity candle." They would each have a lighted candle, and then they would light the single unity candle together. But then what next? The pastor said, "Well, I give you an option. You can either light the unity candle together and then leave your two candles burning, signifying that you are still individuals. Or, you can blow them out, saying we are now *one* in Christ. So, I leave it to you."

And the bride and groom looked at each other and said, "Well, we'll leave them burning. Is that okay?"

The pastor said, "That's fine."

So they came to the ceremony. They came forward, and they said their vows. Then they lifted their candles up, lit the unity candle, and set their candles back in their holders. But then, impishly, the bride leaned over and "whuh!"—the bride blew her husband's candle *out!*

Ken Larson

"I Won the Lottery!"

Ephesians 4:26 "Be angry but do not sin"
Theme: Marriage

One man is talking to another. "My wife and I," he exclaims, "got angry last night and we had a fight." His friend asked him, "How did it end up?" "How did it end up? Why she came crawling to me on her hands and knees!" "What did she say?" "She said, 'Come out from under the bed, you coward!'"

86

That's a veteran vaudeville story. If you want an updated version: the wife called her husband deliriously on the phone. She could hardly catch her breath from the excitement. "Harry," she cried, "I won the lottery! I won the lottery! Pack your clothes!" "Great!" said Harry. "Summer or winter?" "All of them," she said. "I want you out of the house by six!"

Thus anger, hostile and sarcastic—and both different from the anger Jesus displayed in today's Gospel (Jn 2:13-25).

William J. Bausch, *More Telling Stories,* 11

"Are You Really Ready to Get Married?"

Ephesians 5:31 "The two will become one"
Theme: Marriage

(*The following is* not *material for a wedding* sermon(!) *but might be adaptable for a sermon dealing with preparation for marriage.*)

Are you really ready to get married?

Some couples are not.

In the 1950s I was a campus pastor serving the University of California at   Berkeley. We had a   quaint, vine-covered chapel on College Avenue near the campus. Many couples wandered in looking for a place they could use for their wedding.

I remember one couple in particular. He was a "flyboy," a handsome naval pilot based at Alameda Naval Air Station but currently on assignment in Fallon, Nevada. So it was difficult for him to see his fiancee very often, and they had only a little time together on some weekends.

As was my pastoral practice, I counseled them over several months when he was in town. I stressed the unique nature of a Christian marriage. And finally the dates were set for the rehearsal and wedding day.

The rehearsal was on a Friday evening. It went well, in spite of the bride's father being besotted. And afterwards the couple and I met once more, talking about their approaching union.

Saturday afternoon came. The wedding was scheduled for 4:30 p.m. Already at four o'clock many navy brass from Alameda came walking into the chapel. The men were trim in their smart uniforms, their "fruit baskets" (medals) a riot of color below their airmen's wings. Their wives wore elegant furs. It looked to be a festive occasion, and the chapel was full.

I was vested now, ready to begin the service. But...still no bride and groom.

Ten minutes went by. Then another ten. It was now 4:20 p.m. Still no bridal couple. The two families and the assembled congregation looked around expectantly. At that moment, my study phone rang.

It was the "flyboy." "Pastor Deffner? We've been driving around all day, thinking about all the things you've said in our counseling sessions with you. And, you know, we don't think we're really ready to get married." He made a few more comments and then said: "Would you, ah, well, tell the people there that the wedding's off?"

And so it was that I walked down the aisle alone and addressed the congregation. I don't remember my exact words ("Not now...*later!*"). Stunned, looking around at each other, the people gradually left their pews and headed for the rear doors.

I never heard from the couple again.

But in retrospect my primary memory concerning that couple is their *courage*. It took brave resolve to cancel that wedding—and anticipate the talk that would follow on the base. But they had agonized for hours that day. They had confronted the serious realities of a committed Christian marriage. And they felt they were *not ready*.

Are you ready to get married? I pray that you are. I trust that you have met repeatedly with a pastor and worked through the Biblical bases for a lifetime commitment to each other...

Wants or Needs?

Luke 12:15 "Be on your guard against all kinds of greed"
Theme: Materialism

A woman said that all during her life she had made lists of things she wanted. She would always add the date the "want" appeared. But when that particular wish was three months old, she took a look at it again.

Then she asked herself some questions: Did she still want it? Was it of real value? Did she really need it? Could she get along without it?

She noted that during the three-month cooling-off period, more than half of her wants turned out to be temporary whims. They weren't things she really needed.

Adapted from Harold Blake Walker 22

A Dying Daughter

Proverbs 22:6 "Train children in the right way"
Theme: Parenting

A seventeen-year-old girl was dying, due mainly to a rare condition affecting her immune system. She had lost most of her eyesight and her hair as well. But she had a radiant spirit and an infectious smile. At times she became depressed, but after a chat with her pastor she would invariably bounce back.

On the last day of her life she could not sit up or take her medicine. Soon she slipped into a coma. The pastor was sent for, but his car broke down on the 110-mile trip. He felt terrible about it and said he'd call the hospital chaplain.

The mother continues the story:

> After the chaplain left, I got back into Lori's bed and cradled her in my arms. The doctors thought she might be able to hear me, but I was sure she could.
>
> I told her that she was going home today—home to heaven. I told her that Jesus was reaching out his hand to her right now. "I don't want you to be afraid, baby," I said. "Everything is going to be beautiful and perfect. No more pain or I.V.s. No more suffering."
>
> I told her to relax and breathe deep. Stroking and kissing her beautiful bald head, I told her I loved her and wouldn't leave her. She started struggling for breath, and finally breathed her last at 6:41 p.m. I continued holding her for the next two hours, and then I had to say "Good-bye."
>
> I saw Pastor Eatherton the next day at church. He started apologizing again about his car trouble the day before, but when I described Lori's final moments to him, he smiled and said, "I don't feel bad about not being there after all." When I asked why, he said that God must have wanted me to be with Lori at the end. He wanted *me,* the mother, to tell her dying daughter the things I did.
>
> And I understood (Joyce Stacy in *The Lutheran Witness* [June 1992]: 16).

Have you held your child in your arms and told him or her "how to live—and how to die"?

> A moment's space, and gently, wondrously,
> Released from earthly ties,
> Elijah's chariot bears her up to thee,
> Thro' all these lower skies

To yonder shining regions,
While down to meet her come
The blessed angel legions
And bid her welcome home (*The Lutheran Hymnal* 619).

"Walking in Your Steps"

Proverbs 22:6 "Train children in the right way"
Theme: Parenting

A laborer had a day off and decided to spend the time in a bawdy part of town. And so he slipped quietly away from his home and started across a snow-covered field towards his destination. He had not gone far before he heard a voice behind him.

It was his six-year-old son, who said: "Go ahead, Daddy, I'm walking in your steps."

Shocked, the laborer stopped in his tracks. Then he picked his son up in his arms and, collecting his thoughts, said: "Now, what shall we do together today?"

"What's Most Important?"

Matthew 6:19 "Do not store up for yourselves treasures on earth"
Theme: Priorities

A missionary's family in China had been under house arrest, living somewhat comfortably, for years. Well, one day a soldier came in and said, "You can all return to America. But you may take two hundred pounds   with you, no more, no less."

Well, they had been there for years, as I said. Two hundred pounds! So they got the scales and the family arguments started with the husband, wife, and the two children. "Must have this vase. Must have this typewriter; it's almost brand new. Must have these books. Must have this, must have that." And so they weighed each thing and took it off the scale. Weighed it and took it off, until, finally, right on the dot, they got two hundred pounds.

The soldier came the next day and asked, "Ready to go?" They said yes. He said, "Did you weigh everything?" They said yes. "Did you weigh the kids?" "No, we didn't." Weigh the kids," he said. And in a moment, off went the typewriter, off went the books, off went the vase into the trash. The trash. The things that clutter our lives and separate us —into the trash. "Cut it off, pluck it out!" The time has come to decide to put things in perspective. That's the moment you open the door of the present to Jesus.

William J. Bausch, *More Telling Stories*, 4

The Robes of the Christian

Isaiah 61:10 "The robe of righteousness"
Theme: Promises, God's

Ben F. Freudenberg describes one of his "children's sermons."

> The message was prepared for confirmation day. All the young were in their white robes. I used my daughter's baptismal dress and a veil from a wedding dress that one mother had made into their daughter's baptismal gown; the confirmation class in their white robes; the pastor in his white robe; and the funeral pall.
>
> My hope was to tell the children that God's promises or covenants are forever and do not depend on us, that no matter what we do he keeps his promises.
>
> Baptismal Promise by God = Baptismal Robe

Man's Promises = Confirmation Robes, Wedding Robes, Pastor Robes

Not all confirmands stay with their promises.

Not all brides and grooms stay with their promises.

Not all pastors are perfect in staying with their promises.

But the pall, the last white robe, reminds us that God does. No matter how many promises we break, God still will be faithful to us and forgive us through faith given at baptism. We have all he promised through faith, forgiveness, blessed life on earth, and eternal life. The good news is that we have a God that makes a covenant with us, not a contract. No matter what I do, his baptismal promise to me will always stand sure.

A worshiper who first told me about this powerful presentation remarked at how "gripped" the whole congregation was as each robe was commented on. When the ushers finally brought the large funeral pall out from the sacristy into the chancel, a hushed "Oh!" broke forth from the worshipers.

Murphy's Law

James 4:14 "You do not even know what tomorrow will bring"
Theme: Self-Pity

I have a nephew, a real nice Christian young man by the way, who laid careful plans for his sixteenth birthday. He was going to go to school and right after school was going to get his driver's license. He came home from school and, along with his mom and dad, went right down to the motor vehicle department to pay the money and fill out the forms so the birthday boy could drive the family home. The official asked to see his identification. Reaching into his pocket he found that he had forgotten his identification at home. They all rushed home, got what they needed, returned to the motor vehicle office and found that it was closed. Matt was one disappointed young man. His mom had promised to take him out to dinner. The restaurant he planned to go to was—you guessed it—*closed!* Any other suggestions by the birthday boy turned out to be too expensive for the day before payday. They decided to go to a place that the birthday boy could eat for free and then the rest of the family could also afford supper. That restaurant was open and his favorite meal was among the selections available for free birthday meals. He ordered it, but the waitress informed him that they had just run out and he could, however, substitute. *He was really bummed out.*

We have all had days like this, haven't we? When things go like this it is called Murphy's Law: "Every positive action we make demands an equal and nullifying reaction." You know, I planted grass seed and the only place it came up was the cracks in the sidewalk. Murphy's Law happens to careful planners. It has its ultimate effect when sinful, self-centered people make their plans and the rest of the world either intentionally or unintentionally does not feel obliged to go along with them. We have all been foiled when things have not gone our way. It frustrates us. We many times take it out on those that are closest to us. We indulge in self-pity.

Robert Mikkelson

No "Fiascoes"—No Self-Pity

Isaiah 53:4 "Surely he has borne our infirmities"
Theme: Self-Pity

Miss Stella Wood was a pioneer with her kindergarten training school in Minneapolis. Recalling an episode of personal defeat at one point, she wrote to her brother, "I simply loathe the word 'fiasco.' I can look back on a good many of them....And it is unprofitable to think of them long."

She added, "I think that events which do not succeed as we thought they should, should be given to the Lord, as we give our sins....I will not drag along with me like a ball and chain the weaknesses and errors of my past."

The above relates well to the words of evangelist/author Elisabeth Elliot. She had been twice widowed, and one of her insights on how to cope with loneliness was not to be sorry for oneself.

> I try to refuse self-pity. I know of nothing more
> paralyzing, more deadly, than self-pity. It is a death that
> has no resurrection, a sinkhole from which no rescuing
> hand can drag you because you have chosen to sink. But
> it must be refused. In order to refuse it, of course, I must
> recognize it for what it is ("The Ones Who Are Left,"
> *Christianity Today* [February 27, 1976]: 8).

She continues to note the tragic mistake of dwelling on one's own losses or thinking one's own afflictions are unique.

> Christ knows the precise weight and proportion of our
> sufferings—*he bore them.* He carried our sorrows. He
> suffered, wrote George MacDonald, not that we might
> not suffer, but that our sufferings might be like his. To
> hell, then, with self-pity.

Adapted from Harold Blake Walker 46

Some Tasty German Pastries

Galatians 6:10 "Let us work for the good of all"
Theme: Service

Some years ago some Jewish refugees in Mexico expressed a desire for German pastries. The pastries weren't essential, but they would be a tasty treat. Dr. Oswald Golter, a missionary to Mexico, went to extra trouble and expense to get the pastries to give to these refugees.

"But why did you do that?" someone protested. "They don't even believe in Jesus."

Golter responded, "But I do."

The Big Offering

Mark 12:44 "She...put in everything she had"
Theme: Stewardship

Several years ago, Dr. Robert Thomas heard that a community of poor people in the Great Smoky Mountains region of Tennessee were in desperate need of medical help. He decided to go and try to help them. He was a devout Christian; and, soon, the people began looking to him for help not only with their medical needs, but their other problems as well. On one occasion, Dr. Thomas was called out to a settlement known as Brown Mare Hollow. The Walker family lived there and young Billy Walker had the measles. After Dr. Thomas treated Billy, he asked his parents whether or not their ten children were receiving any Christian instruction. They told him that the people on their side of the mountain had no church and could manage only occasionally to get over to the other side where there was a church. A short time later, Dr. Thomas called a meeting of all the people living there. He suggested they fix up an old cabin and use it for their church.

With great excitement they did so. When they had finished, they asked Dr. Thomas to be their preacher until they could find one. He agreed to do so.

When Sunday came, the poor people of Brown Mare Hollow gathered for worship. They sang and prayed with great enthusiasm. Then Dr. Thomas preached his first sermon. "Never," he said, "was there a more attentive congregation." When the sermon had ended, Dr. Thomas began to dismiss the people. But little Billy Walker stood and said, "Doc, you're forgettin' somethin'!" "What is it?" the doctor asked. "You're forgettin' the collection," the young lad said. Dr. Thomas was stunned. He had no intention of taking an offering. These were very poor people. But he could sense that all of the congregation wanted to do something. They knew that the experience of God's presence in their worship called for nothing less than their total response. And so Billy's hat was passed and the offering was taken. After the service, Dr. Thomas went out and sat in his car, prayerfully considering what he had just experienced. He counted the money and wrote on the envelope: "Brown Mare Hollow congregation—13 cents."

Timothy Sims

The Elderly Man on the Floor

Leviticus 19:34 "The alien...shall be to you as the citizen among you"
Theme: Strangers, Welcoming

In *Out of the Salt Shaker and into the World*, Rebecca Manley Pippert tells of a church that wanted to reach out to students at the nearby university. But the church had a well-dressed, middle-class clientele of members.

One Sunday a student visited the church. He came in blue jeans and a T-shirt, but with no shoes. The church was crowded down to the last pew. Finding no seat, he walked down the aisle and just squatted on the carpet. The tension was so thick you could slice it.

Then an elderly man walked down the aisle. What would he do? Everyone watched him. With great difficulty he lowered himself down to the floor and sat next to the young man for the rest of the service.

"I was told there was not a dry eye in the congregation," says Pippert.

The Thirteenth Suicide

Mark 10:21 "Jesus, looking at him, loved him"
Theme: Suicide

Last week I went back to a little graduation party at Boston College. And when I was up there I picked up the *Boston Globe* and read, to my sadness, that another kid up at M.I.T. jumped off the thirteenth story of a building and killed himself. Out of a possible 4.0, a perfect score, he was a student who got 3.96. He was a genius, but he still felt inadequate. And then, of course, you have all the outpourings in the editorials. Well, he was the thirteenth one to commit suicide since this school year began.

The editorials talk about the unrelenting move for technical excellence and for achievement. They point to the fact that these hyper schools like M.I.T. are scientifically probably the best in the world. That's all important, but the real issue is whether we make room for the humanness of the student. The important thing is whether we say, "Hey, if you are not perfect we still love you. Your worth is not tied up in getting the best marks so that the greatest engineering corporation in the world will pick you up and start you out at $50,000 a year. Even if you don't get that job, *you* are *who* you are, the very image and likeness of God. And God loves you deeply."

William J. Bausch, *Timely Homilies*, 85-86

"Get Off My Boat!"

Matthew 4:10 "Away with you, Satan!"
Theme: Temptation

During the Civil War it was illegal to trade in cotton. But many unscrupulous speculators tried to buy cotton in the South, run it through the Union lines, and sell it at great profit in the North.

One of these speculators approached a Mississippi steamboat captain and offered him $100 if he would run his cotton up the river for him. The captain declined, reminding him it was illegal.

"I will give you $500," said the man.

"No," answered the captain.

"I will give you $1,000."

"No," the captain said again.

"I will give you $3,000!"

At that the captain drew his pistol, and pointing it at the man, said, "Get off this boat! You are coming too near my price!"

What is *your* "price"?

A Mother Crying Piteously

Romans 5:3 "Suffering produces endurance"
Theme: Testing

It was the dead of winter in western Montana. A woman and her child were crossing the frozen prairies in a bus. They were the only passengers besides the driver.

It was bitterly cold. But what was worse, the bus's heating system had failed. And the driver realized that the mother was gradually becoming unconscious from the cold.

So he suddenly did a strange thing. He stopped the bus, grabbed the baby from the mother's arms and, wrapping it warmly, placed it underneath the seat.

Then he seized the mother by the arm, dragged her outside, and drove away, leaving her in the freezing snow.

Stupefied, the mother saw the bus leaving, and ran after it, crying piteously for her baby.

When the bus driver was sure the mother's blood circulation was going again, he allowed her to overtake the bus. He opened the door and restored the child to the mother's outstretched arms.

Only then did she realize that he had saved her life.

Often God permits severe spiritual tests to come to our lives. But then—and sometimes only then—are we restored to faithful, vigorous Christian living.

"Mommy, I'm Scared"

Joshua 1:5 "I will not fail you or forsake you
Theme: Trust

A burst of thunder sent a three-year-old flying into her parents' bedroom. "Mommy, I'm scared," she said.

The mother, half-awake and half-unconscious, replied, "Go back to your room. God will be there with you."

The small figure stood in the unlit doorway for a moment and then said softly, "Mommy, I'll sleep here with Daddy and you go in there and sleep with God."

Dynamic Preaching 7, no. 8 [August 1992]: 6

Her "Professional Worrier"

1 Peter 1:8 "Although you have not seen him, you love him"
Theme: Trust

The secret of knowing joy in life—even in suffering—is in a growing vibrant relationship with Christ. Even when the situation dictates otherwise.

I met a young girl that had this experience of Christian joy. She worked at the hardware store and her husband had just lost his job. The woman who worked with her had been watching her handle the situation and after a few days came up to her and said, "I've been watching you and you have every reason to be angry and upset by what happened to you. But you have peace about you that I can't understand. What do you have that I don't have?" My friend said that she thought about it for a little while and said that she had a "professional worrier" doing her worrying for her. She went on to explain that she had a personal relationship with the risen Christ.

This honest response opened the door for a sharing of Jesus and what he did on the cross. That's when tears of joy appeared in her eyes. She knew that Jesus was using her and her situation to bring this friend to Jesus.

She had a totally different view of what was going on in her life compared to her fellow workers. She saw that the world, and her flesh, and the devil were bidding for her attention. Their desire was for her to take her eyes off of the author and finisher of her faith. The world and our flesh can only give us temporary happiness. Real happiness comes by being with Jesus every day.

Her motto was "I know there is a God. I know he is up to something. And guess what? I know I'm included." *Wow!* Can anything come close in this world to being part of God's plans? *God!* The creator of the universe and all that is in it is your friend and loves you dearly.

Peter spoke of this personal relationship with the Lord that we have. Listen to him speak of this relationship: "Without having seen him you love him; though you do not now see him you believe in him and rejoice with unutterable and exalted joy. As the outcome of your faith you obtain the salvation of your souls" (1 Pet 1:8).

Phil Found

"Put Your Arms around My Neck"

Deuteronomy 33:27 (KJV) "Underneath are the everlasting arms"
Mark 10:16 "And he took them up in his arms"
Theme: Trust

In the TV movie *Eric,* the young boy Eric is struggling with cancer. There is a touching moment when the boy and his father stand on the beach by their summer cottage. Eric says, "Daddy, remember how I wanted to swim across the bay with you? We got halfway across and I said I couldn't make it. You reached out and held onto me. Remember? Well, Daddy, I don't think I can make it now." Eric's father quietly spreads his arms around him and says, "I won't let you go down. Put your arms around my neck, and we'll go on together."

We don't know what 1992 will bring. Most likely there will be times when we feel as if we have been ripped off. There will be situations when we think we have been treated unjustly. There will be hurtful times when, like little Eric, we think we are going down and there is no hope. As Peter says, we feel like straying sheep who have lost their way.

Yet there is someone who puts his arms around us. There is one who gave his life for us and who promises to go with us in this new year. There is one who gives real and lasting hope in hurtful times: our Good Shepherd, Jesus Christ.

May God help us to trust in the Lord Jesus Christ, our Good Shepherd, so we keep returning to him. He is our true hope in hurtful times.

Luther C. Brunette

"God, You Take Over"

1 Peter 5:7 "Cast all your anxieties on him"
Theme: Trust

A woman had suffered a lot of agony over her daughter's unfulfilled life. The suffering the daughter had gone through she made her own. But the painful identification with her girl's difficulties had not subsided until she came to the realization, as she put it: "Two weeks ago I finally gave up on worrying about my daughter's problems. I finally turned them over to God. I said, 'Here, God, you take over. I can't handle it any more.' "

That was obedience—in resignation to God. That was looking unto him in all things and knowing he is able to do that which we are unable to do. At this moment, that mother has seen no immediate change in her girl's life. But the mother has an inner peace she didn't have before, for she learned to obey Christ's words: "If you love me keep my commandments"—the commandment to "cast all your cares on me, for I care for you."

Donald L. Deffner, *Bound to Be Free,* 88

Condition: Critical

Deuteronomy 33:27 (KJV) "Underneath are the everlasting arms"
Theme: Trust

A friend of mine tells of how, years ago, he was in a horrible car accident. His car was totaled, and he woke up for the first time after the crash in a hospital bed. There was no one in the room at the time, so he felt himself gingerly all over and then looked around the room. Over on the windowsill was a chart, and he carefully got out of bed and walked over to look at it. He read his name, and then "Condition: critical." Me? Critical? he thought. He crept even more carefully back to bed and leaning back slowly took stock of his situation. "Well, there's absolutely nothing I can do about it. So I throw myself completely in your hands, Lord. Do what you wish." He says he never felt such a complete sense of relief and joyful daring as he took the "leap of faith" into God's hands and laid back to relax in the safe care of the everlasting arms.

He calls that feeling, which he has sought to practice throughout his life, his "theology of failure." In life's circumstances you trust, you leap, you dare to fail, to lose, to miss out. But at least in God's name, you dared.

Donald L. Deffner, *Bound to Be Free,* 117

"The Canoe Is Sinking!"

Acts 2:44 "[They] had all things in common"
Theme: Unity

The waters of the Bourbois River boiled angrily. Our canoe careened from shoreline to shoreline, striking the boulders that lurked beneath the water. We lurched downstream this way for most of the morning.

My friend and I, green to the ways of the river, spent much of our time ducking to avoid being clotheslined by the branches that overhung the channel. We expended much of our energy bemoaning the fact that we had not postponed our trip a few days to allow the river, now swollen by last weekend's rains, to calm down. We poured the rest of our effort into paddling—albeit unskillfully—away from the massive rocks that dotted the riverbed.

Around noon, we began to relax and to congratulate ourselves that the thuds we had encountered with such great regularity in the beginning were now jarring us much less often. I began to paddle with more assurance, looking downstream to check for future hazards and feeling a little like Mark Twain himself.

Just then my friend cleared her throat. "Excuse me," she said, "but your end of the canoe is sinking!"

We hear the cliche often—"We are all in this together." Cliches usually become cliches because everyone recognizes the nuggets of truth embedded in them. Especially as we work with others on a staff-team to serve Christ and his people, we share the same canoe. We paddle and float together, or we founder and sink together.

Jane Fryar 187

"Life's a Battle"

Ephesians 6:11 "Put on the whole armor of God"
Theme: Warfare, Spiritual

This could only happen in Texas. Two sons bought their elderly mother a gun to carry because they were worried about her safety. "We wanted to be comfortable that mother would be able to protect herself should she ever be attacked in these uncertain times," they related to the *Dallas Daily News*. "We taught her how to use it. We were not irresponsible."

Mom dutifully packed her gift rod in her purse. One day, as she left the Ridgmar Shopping Center, getting into the car she found two young men sitting in the front seat. Pulling out her new "peacemaker," she screamed, "Get out of my car or I'll shoot and kill you!" The frightened duo jumped out of the car and ran off.

Mom got in, put the key in the ignition and *it didn't fit*. She now knew the truth. She was in the *wrong car*. She saw her car sitting in the very *next* row. She said that she would like to make an apology "to those boys, if it's not too late."

Life's a battle, always a struggle. People defending themselves, sometimes from people that they have mistaken for their enemies.

Eddie Balfour

Latter Sundays
of Ordinary Time
(Season after Pentecost)

The Advent season, of course, included a penitential tone with the propers, indicating the need to be ready for our Lord's advent at the end of time. But this theme is also picked up on the lessons at the end of Ordinary Time (Season after Pentecost). Accordingly, illustrations referring to death are placed in this section.

"Give Me Tomorrow"

Hebrews 9:27 "It is appointed for mortals to die once"
Theme: Death

Marguerite Higgins was a woman war correspondent in Korea. One day, in the dead of winter, she was visiting an area where marines were taking a much-needed rest. They had been on the front lines without winter clothing and were fighting a Red Chinese army that outnumbered the marines ten to one.

She came across one big, tough marine who was seated on the ground eating out of a can. His body was slumped from lack of sleep and his eyes were bloodshot. The moisture on his beard was frozen. She walked up to him and asked him if she could give him anything. His answer was, "Give me tomorrow."

Timothy Sims

Singing Yourself to Death

2 Timothy 1:12 "I know the one in whom I have put my trust"
Theme: Death

Few people know that the Gloria Patri ("Glory be to the Father and to the Son and to the Holy Ghost") which many of us sing in our churches every Sunday was really based on the death-march song of the early Christian martyrs. They knew they would die, but they faced their end with conviction, knowing "whom they had believed and...persuaded that he was able to keep that which they had committed unto him against that day."

Donald L. Deffner, *Bound to Be Free*, 118

The Ship on the Horizon

1 Corinthians 13:12 "Then we will see face to face"
Theme: Death

Picture yourself standing on a dock watching a great sailing ship waiting silently and quietly for a wind to fill its sails and set it in majestic motion. Finally, a strong wind comes up and all spring into action. The captain shouts orders, the sailors hoist the great sails, the wind catches them with a great puff, and off the ship slowly moves like a giant sea serpent on the waters. But by and by the ship grows smaller and smaller as it eventually becomes but a speck where sky and sea meet on the horizon. Someone on the dock shouts the traditional cry, "There she goes!" and everyone waves good-bye and goes home.

But the question is, "Goes where?" That ship which is just a little dot on our horizon is just as big and mighty, just as laden with cargo and people as it was on the dock. The difference is in us. The difference is that it has merely receded from our sight and disappeared, that's all. But somewhere, as it moves to a foreign shore, that dot, that tiny ship, invisible to us, becomes larger and larger. And there are people on that foreign shore who are about to set up a new cry. They shout, "There she comes!"

William J. Bausch, *More Telling Stories*, 146-147

Facing Death

1 Corinthians 13:12 "Then we will see face to face"

Theme: Death

How can I face death, God?

God responds:

Proud and High in the Water

You think your friend
is dead and gone?
In one sense you are wrong
For though you saw that friend
on the shore of life
like a vessel
with a full head of sail
and then that ship
moved farther away until
it was only a speck
on the horizon
and then vanished
I from the other shore
saw that speck become
a full-masted vessel again
proud and high in the water
Now berthed here in my harbor
together we look forward
to the day
when another vessel appears
on the horizon
Yours

Donald L. Deffner, *Come Closer*, 52

Just a Visitor

Hebrews 13:14 "Here we have no lasting city"
Theme: Death, Preparation for

A man once visited a well-known clergyman. But he was astonished to see that his home was only a simple room filled with books. The only furniture was a table and a bench.

· "Where is your furniture?" asked the tourist in amazement.

"Where is yours?" replied the clergyman.

"Mine? But I'm only a visitor here."

"So am I," came the response.

Adapted from Anthony DeMello, *Song of the Bird,* 137

Three Surprises

Ephesians 2:8 "For by grace you have been saved"
Theme: Heaven

C. S. Lewis once noted that when we get to heaven, there will be three surprises: First, we will be surprised by the people that we find there, many of whom we surely had not expected to see. The second surprise is that we will be surprised by the people who are absent—the ones we did expect to see but who are not there. The third surprise, of course, will be that we're there.

William J. Bausch, *More Telling Stories,* 72

Christ the King/Last Sunday of Ordinary Time (Season after Pentecost)

On this day we celebrate the rule of Christ as King over all creation. We pray that all people, now divided by the power of sin, may be united under the glorious and gentle rule of our blessed Lord.

The Burning Barn

Romans 8:32 "But gave him up for all of us"
Theme: Christ

Back in Minnesota where I come from, there is a lonely country road that winds past an old farm. On that farm, close to the road, is a white shed that is the pride and joy of the owner. You see, he built the building himself.

Well, late one Friday night a couple of high school students who had just passed their driver's test came driving through. As they drove past the farm the headlights of the car lit up one side of the beautiful white shed (as beautiful as sheds get, anyway). Suddenly, the students got a great idea. They pulled the car into a field road a few hundred feet down the road. Then in silence the students ran back to the shed and with spray paint in hand began to spray obscenities all over the white building.

The next morning the owner woke up and looked out his window in dismay. He couldn't believe that anyone could be that cruel. However, over the next several days he repainted his shed and once again it was back to top-notch shape.

But then another Friday night came around and the same students came driving by with another plan. They parked in the same spot and ran back to the shed; however, this time they didn't bring spray paint. In the darkness, they found the door and entered the building. Once inside, they began pouring gasoline all over the walls and floor and then lit a match. The problem was that in their excitement they had failed to realize that the latch on the door was rusty and had a problem with getting stuck. And so they found themselves locked in a burning building that was quickly becoming deadly. Frantically they pounded on the walls trying to find a way out, but the smoke and heat soon became too much for them and they gasped for a last breath of air on the floor. The next thing they knew they were being thrown out the door by a man. At the same time the roof fell in and trapped him in the flames. However, the students escaped unharmed.

The next day the remains of a man were found in the ashes and were identified to be the owner. He gave up his life for them.

And Christ gave up his life for you. He loved you that much.

Of course, our story doesn't end here. Christ rose again on the third day and overcame death for you. There is no reason to hide anymore. Death is no longer something to be feared, bur rather something to anticipate with great joy! By his love you are indeed forgiven—completely.

Marc Schwichtenberg

Hooked Up to Christ

John 15:5 "Apart from me you can do nothing"
Theme: Christ

The six-month night at the South Pole must have seemed endless to Admiral Richard E. Byrd, even though he had provided himself with a small hut and all the necessities of life. One day he wandered away into a snowstorm. Suddenly he realized he could no longer see the smokestack of his little home. What to do? First he was determined not to panic. Second, he decided to mark the spot so that he didn't wander off farther into the wrong direction. He hammered a stake into the ice and attached a long rope to it. Then, in ever-widening circles he moved out around the peg until he got so far he almost pulled the peg loose. He went back, refastened it to the ice, and added another section of rope. This time as he circled around the peg he walked directly into the door of his little hut. He had found his way.

We can learn from that. No matter how far we may have wandered on our own, when we become firmly attached to

Christ by a God-empowered faith that holds on tenaciously, we will find our way through life with the Savior's leading.

Mark E. Gilson

That Striking Face

**Revelation 7:14 "They have washed their robes
and made them white in the blood of the Lamb"
Theme: Christ**

Frederick Buechner, the author, recalls the inescapable impact that the holy face of Jesus had on him during his wild days of youth. His father had committed suicide when Frederick was just a little boy. In order to provide the best for him, his mother sent him to a prestigious boarding school. He was often lonely, so he found adventure by looking through books of art. One day he saw the most perfect face he could imagine. This face was the epitome of love, compassion, strength, and kindness. The face was Leonardo DaVinci's sketch of Jesus for his well-known painting, *The Last Supper.* Frederick did not know the first thing about who Jesus is, or what he did, but he knew from the sketch that Jesus was like no other person.

One night, while carousing with some of his friends, Frederick heard Jesus' name spoken amidst a string of foul and vulgar words. He immediately felt dirty and unclean from hearing and seeing Jesus' holy face dragged through the sewer. He frantically ran through the town in search of an open church where he could see Jesus' face washed clean in his mind. It didn't stop there, for Frederick's sins were eventually washed clean in the waters of baptism. God looked at Frederick and saw the work of his Son Jesus Christ who had washed him clean.

Jesus is the Son who worked in the vineyard for us. Our entrance into the kingdom of God does not depend on our most outstanding achievements, or our most despicable failures for that matter. Our entrance into the kingdom of God depends upon the work of Jesus. We cannot do the will of God, but Jesus came down from heaven not to do his will but the will of the Father who sent him. Jesus said, "The will of the Father is that everyone who sees the Son and believes in him shall have eternal life."

Joel R. Kurz

Two Birds in the Church

John 8:36 "If the Son makes you free, you will be free indeed"
Theme: Christ, Freedom in

A church organist writes: It was a warm summer day for the wedding so the doors of our non-air-conditioned church were left standing open. As I was playing the pre-nuptial music, two birds suddenly flew in through the open front door. The dome of our nave being quite high, the birds immediately flew to the highest areas of the nave looking for a way to freedom. They continued to fly frantically during the wedding, causing distraction. At the end of the service, I tried to approach the creatures which now at times rested momentarily from their efforts, but each time I approached them, they flew upward against ceilings and walls far beyond the reach of any net. Unless they changed their minds and stopped their own efforts and let me near them to rescue them and carry them to freedom, they would eventually die in this manmade structure of religion, this self-imposed religious prison of their choosing.

As time passed, one bird sought the highest point in this manmade religious structure and entered the false security of the highest organ pipe where he died with one wing hanging out of the mouth of the organ pipe beyond anyone's reach to remove him after his death. Perhaps he could be called the "lawyer bird" because that bird never had a change of mind and never stopped insisting on his own method of rescue, just as the lawyer in the parable of the Good Samaritan, from what we know, never had a change of mind and never stopped insisting on being saved by his own efforts. Of such people Jesus said in John 8:24, "...you will die in your sins." How sad! How hopeless!

And then a rescue of the remaining bird was made possible. A container of food and water was set out. The bird was drawn to it. This allowed for it to be netted. Its bruises were cleaned and it was carried to the open door to freedom where it could again live as the creature that God intended it to be.

Can you see the events of *your* life in this second bird? While we were fluttering about in our vain attempts for freedom from fear through our efforts to fulfill the Law, God's Spirit set out for us the "food" of his Gospel Word. This turned our minds and efforts, and as we ate of the food of his Word, the Spirit netted us into the net of God's kingdom and family where our bruises from sin were washed in the waters of baptism. He led us to Christ who is the door to true freedom. For Jesus himself has said, "If you continue in my word, you are truly my disciples, and you will know the truth, and the truth will make you free" (Jn 8:31-32). And "...if the Son makes you free, you will be free indeed" (Jn 8:36).

Merlin D. Holtzen

The God Who "Shows Through"

Matthew 5:16 "Let your light shine before others"
1 John 4:17 "As he is, so are we in this world"
Theme: Christ the Indwelling

Daughter: "Daddy, I am having a problem understanding God. Is God really all over the world?"

Father: "Yes, daughter. God is everywhere. He is there *for us.*"

Daughter: "In other words, Daddy, God is *huge!* Daddy, you also told me that God is *in* me, in my *heart?*"

Father: "Yes, daughter, God is truly in our hearts and loves us."

Daughter: "Well, Daddy, if God's *that* huge and also in my heart, won't he be showing through?"

James L. Voigtmann

"Don't Let Him Drown!"

Galatians 2:20 "It is no longer I who live,
but it is Christ who lives in me"
Theme: Christ the Savior

Watchman Nee tells of the time he stood on a dock by a lake. Beside him was a friend who was an excellent swimmer. Suddenly they saw a man in trouble in the water. Soon he screamed for help.

"Aren't you going to help him?!" Nee asked his friend anxiously.

"Not yet," he calmly replied.

Soon the man kept going under, and he was fighting for air.

"Save him!" Nee begged.

"Not yet," his friend said again.

Finally, the man disappeared and Nee's friend instantly dove in and dragged him to shore. Soon he was revived. Then Nee asked why he hadn't acted earlier.

"I had no choice," the man said calmly. "If I'd gone to him immediately he would have panicked and pulled me down. I had to wait until he stopped kicking. Then I could save him."

Are you willing to stop kicking? Are you willing to see all your little problems and unresolved conflicts, discouragements and disappointments, bad habits, negative attitudes, faults, and failures as being means whereby God is at work bringing you to the end of yourself? Are you willing to be nailed to the cross of Christ and buried in the waters of your baptism?

Get off yourself! You are the problem. Reject yourself! Forget about yourself. You are beyond help. God has given to you Jesus who is your help. C. S. Lewis writes at the very end of *Mere Christianity*:

> Look for yourself, and you will find in the long run only
> hatred, loneliness, despair, rage, ruin, and decay. But
> look for Christ and you will find him, and with him
> everything else thrown in.

Adapted from Matzat 82-83

Learning How to Plow

Hebrews 13:8 "Jesus Christ is the same"
Theme: Christ the Unchangeable

A farmer was trying to teach his son how to plow a straight furrow. After the horse had been hitched up and all was ready, he told the boy to keep an eye on some object at the other end of the field and aim straight toward it.

"Do you see that cow way out there?" he asked. "Keep your eye on her, and plow straight ahead."

The boy started plowing and the farmer went back to do his chores. When he returned sometime later to see what progress had been made, he was shocked to find instead of a straight row something that looked like a question mark.

"What happened?" he shouted. Well, the boy had obeyed the instruction of his father. But the cow had moved.

Christ is the one who never changes. He is the foundation of our faith. He is the cornerstone, the faithful rock who is unmovable. When we set our eyes on him, our path will be straight.

OTHER FEASTS
& OCCASIONAL
SERVICES

All Saints Day

Nothing More Beyond?

John 11:25 "I am the resurrection and the life"
Theme: All Saints Day

Centuries ago the Spanish fleet had the following inscription on their flags: NON PLUS ULTRA—"Nothing More Beyond." But then Columbus discovered America, and they had to remove the "NON" from their flags. Then the flags read: PLUS ULTRA—"More Beyond."

There is "more beyond." Today we remember "All Saints" who have died "in the Lord" and think of the day we shall join them. For there is "more beyond." As our Lord Jesus Christ said: "I am the resurrection and the life; [those] who believe in me, even though [they] die, yet shall live, and whoever lives and believes in me shall never die" (Jn 11:25-26).

Thanksgiving

Although Thanksgiving is not in the liturgical calendar, the following vignette relating to it is included because of the singular importance of that day in our national history and heritage.

Thankfulness

Philippians 4:6 "In everything...with thanksgiving"
Theme: Thanksgiving

The year 1991 was a very good one for former President George Bush. He faced a very difficult situation when Iraq invaded Kuwait. He promised to free Kuwait one way or another, using sanctions first; and if they failed, he told Saddam Hussein, force would be used. Well, we all know what happened next. Using an unlikely military coalition, the allied troops routed Iraq's army in short order, and Kuwait was liberated. President Bush was looked at as a hero after the Gulf War, with his approval rating at an astounding 90 percent. But what a difference a year can make. Within one year the American people decided that they no longer wanted President Bush to lead them for four more years. When it came to the election, its as if they were asking President Bush, "What have you done for us lately?"

And if you and I are honest with each other, we must admit that this is exactly the same way that we oftentimes treat God. Have we ever forgotten to give God thanks for the many blessings that he has given to us? Do we in fact fail to recognize that all that we have is given to us from God?

"What has God done for you lately?" Although we are often times disloyal to God, he will always provide us with all of our physical and spiritual needs.

Paul J. Mundinger

References

Each illustration in this book is followed by the name of its author (if no name is given, the illustration is my own and has not been previously published). Some illustrations are reprinted from other sources; their full bibliographic information is given here. If no further information is provided, the illustration most likely came from the homilist in the seminary classroom or in the parish.

Aho, Gerhard et al. *Lent: A Time for Renewal*. St. Louis: Concordia, 1989.

Anderson, Richard, and Donald L. Deffner. *For Example: Illustrations for Contemporary Preaching*. St. Louis: Concordia, 1977.

Bausch, William J. *More Telling Stories, Compelling Stories*. Mystic, Connecticut: Twenty-Third Publications, 1993.

———. *Timely Homilies: The Wit and Wisdom of an Ordinary Pastor*. Mystic, Connecticut: Twenty-Third Publications, 1990.

Brunette, Luther C. "Hope for Hurtful Times." *Concordia Pulpit Resources* 2, part 1 (Advent 1991- Transfiguration 1992): 61.

Deffner, Donald L. *Bound to Be Free*. Seattle: Morse Press, 1981. Reprint Fort Wayne, Indiana: Concordia Theological Seminary Press, 1992.

———. *Bold Ones on Campus*. Out of print.

———. *The Best of Your Life Is the Rest of Your Life*. Out of print.

———. *Come Closer to Me, God!* St. Louis: Concordia, 1982.

———. *Compassionate Preaching: A Primer/Primer in Homiletics*. Fort Wayne, Indiana: Concordia Theological Seminary Press, 1991.

————. *The Possible Years: Thoughts after Thirty on Christian Adulthood.* Out of print.

————. "Preaching to the Educated." *The Compassionate Mind: Theological Dialog with the Educated.* St. Louis: Concordia, 1990.

Deffner, Donald L., et al. *Sermon Illustrations for the Gospel Lessons.* St. Louis: Concordia, 1980.

DeMello, Anthony. *The Song of the Bird.* Garden City, New Jersey: Doubleday, 1984.

Dubberke, Edwin. "Praise God from A to Z." *Concordia Pulpit Resources* 2, part 1 (1977): 23.

Fryar, Jane. *Go and Make Disciples.* St. Louis: Concordia, 1992.

Fuller, David Otis, ed. *Spurgeon's Sermon Notes.* Grand Rapids: Zondervan Publishing House, 1941.

Gaulke, Stephen. "Just for You." *Teachers Interaction* (December 1993): 12.

Hoover, David W. "Focus on the Nativity." *Concordia Pulpit Resources* 2, part 1 (Advent 1991 - Transfiguration 1992): 23.

Kempis, Thomas à. *The Imitation of Christ.* Rockland, Maine: Dunstan Press, 1985.

Kirklin, Suzanne Swartz. "Changing Spots." *Teachers Interaction* (December 1991): 1.

Kolb, Peter. "Christmas Frees from Chains." *The Osceola Sentinel* (December 21, 1990).

Lang, P. H. D. *Ceremony and Celebration.* St. Louis: Concordia, 1965.

Lowry, Eugene L. *The Homiletical Plot.* Atlanta: John Knox Press, 1980.

Matzat, Don. *Christ Esteem.* Eugene, Oregon: Harvest House, 1990.

Murdaugh, George. "Shedding Some Light." *The Lutheran Witness* (June 1992): 22.

Nelson, Wilbur E. *Anecdotes and Illustrations.* Grand Rapids, Michigan: Baker, 1971.

Nes, William H. *Preaching in Lent.* New York: Charles Scribner's Sons, 1957.

Pippert, Rebecca Manley. *Out of the Salt Shaker and into the World.* Downers Grove, Illinois: InterVarsity Press, 1979.

Sandmann, Donald W. "An Encounter with Hope." *Concordia Pulpit Resources* (1988): 93-94.

Stacy, Joyce. "I'd Know What to Do." *The Lutheran Witness* (June 1992): 16.

Walker, Harold Blake. *Heart of the Christian Year.* New York: Harper and Bros., 1961.

Wolber, David. *Getting Ready for Christmas.* Minneapolis: Augsburg, 1969.

More Resources for Preachers and Teachers

HOMILY RESOURCES from *Celebrating the Lectionary*
edited by Liz Montes
Looseleaf, 312 pages, 8½" x 11"

Helpful reflections on the Sunday readings that help you think without telling you what to think. Use independently or coordinate with the CTL curriculum. Covers every Sunday of the year from the first Sunday in September through the last Sunday in August each year. Published annually.

SEASONAL ILLUSTRATIONS FOR PREACHING AND TEACHING
Donald L. Deffner
Paper, 176 pages, 5½" x 8½", ISBN 0-89390-234-9

Preachers and teachers: use these illustrations to get your listeners' attention and enrich their understanding of the church year.

SERMONS FOR SERMON HATERS
Andre Papineau
Paper, 144 pages, 5½" x 8½", ISBN 0-89390-229-2

It's a preacher's dream—to turn on the turned-off. Andre Papineau shows you how to break open the Gospel in ways that reach even the most jaded.

THE DREAM CATCHER: 20 Lectionary-Based Stories for Teaching and Preaching
James L. Henderschedt
Paper, 128 pages, 5½" x 8½", ISBN 0-89390-339-6

"Clever, poignant, humorous, in touch with our human reality, his stories, once read, are not the end, but rather the beginning of insight into my journey toward a loving God..." — Father Edward Miller, pastor, St. Bernardine's Catholic Church

Call 1-800-736-7600 for current prices.
See last page for ordering information.

More Resources for Preachers and Teachers

STORYTELLING STEP BY STEP

Marsh Cassady, PhD

Paper, 156 pages, 5½" x 8½", ISBN 0-89390-183-0

Marsh Cassady, a director, actor, and storyteller, shows you all the steps to successful storytelling: selecting the right story for your audience, adapting your story for different occasions, analyzing it so that you can present it well, preparing your audience, and presenting the story. Includes many examples of stories.

CREATING STORIES FOR STORYTELLING

Marsh Cassady, PhD

Paper, 144 pages, 5½" x 8½", ISBN 0-89390-205-5

This book picks up where the author's popular *Storytelling Step-by-Step* left off. Includes ideas for creating your own original stories, adapting stories to different audiences, plotting a story, creating tension, and writing dialogue that will keep your listeners on the edge of their chairs.

CREATIVE STORYTELLING

Marsh Cassady, PhD

three audiocassettes

These audiocassettes are adapted from the author's books *Storytelling Step-by-Step* and *Creating Stories for Storytelling*. Learn all the steps to successful storytelling: selecting the right story for your audience, adapting your story for different occasions and audiences, analyzing it, preparing your audience, and presenting the story. You'll also find ideas for creating your own original stories, plotting a story, creating tension, and writing dialogue that will keep your listeners on the edge of their chairs. The author's theatrical experience helps the example stories take on a life of their own.

Call 1-800-736-7600 for current prices.
See last page for ordering information.

More Resources for Preachers and Teachers

STORY AS A WAY TO GOD: A Guide for Storytellers
H. Maxwell Butcher

Paper, 153 pages, 5½" x 8½", ISBN 0-89390-201-2

Why are stories so powerful? This book reveals the dynamics of good storytelling. Find out why every good story from "The Ugly American" to "West Side Story" says something about the divine. Learn how to find God's story everywhere—and how to tell it.

NO KIDDING, GOD, WHERE ARE YOU? Parables of Ordinary Experience
Lou Ruoff

Paper, 106 pages, 5½" x 8½", ISBN 0-89390-141-5

The author shows you where he finds God: in a bottle of whiteout, in a hand of poker, in a game of hopscotch. These twenty-five stories work effectively as homilies and as ways to find God in everyday life. To help you with your planning, they are accompanied by Scripture references according to the season of the liturgical year.

PARABLES OF BELONGING: Discipleship and Commitment in Everyday Life
Lou Ruoff

Paper, 112 pages, 5½" x 8½", ISBN 0-89390-253-5

The collection of stories in *Parables of Belonging* recognizes the ability of average people to minister to others in their lives just by carrying out their day-to-day activities. Telling these stories will help listeners acknowledge and rejoice in their own "hidden" giftedness and invigorate your community.

Call 1-800-736-7600 for current prices.
See last page for ordering information.

More Resources for Preachers and Teachers

STORY POWER! Compelling Illustrations for Preaching and Teaching

James A. Feehan

Paper, 120 pages, 5½" x 8½", ISBN 0-89390-304-3

To really get your point across, you've got to tell stories. Good ones. Short ones. Powerful ones. Stories that intrigue. Stories that fascinate. Stories that capture the imagination. And then—since you're not just in the entertainment business—your stories have to hook your listeners to the Gospel message. A tall order. This book by famed Irish preacher James Feehan will help. It's packed with dozens of anecdotes, quick story illustrations, and great tips for more powerful storytelling. A must for preachers and teachers.

PARABLES FOR LITTLE PEOPLE
Paper, 101 pages, 5½" x 8½", ISBN 0-89390-034-6

MORE PARABLES FOR LITTLE PEOPLE
Paper, 82 pages, 5½" x 8½", ISBN 0-89390-095-8

both by Lawrence Castagnola

With imaginative parables, Castagnola's positive message helps reach children in preaching, in teaching, and in the simple pleasures of storytelling. Sixteen parables in the first volume, and fifteen more in the second.

Order from your local bookseller, or contact:

Resource Publications, Inc.
160 E. Virginia Street #290
San Jose, CA 95112-5876
1-800-736-7600 (voice)
1-408-287-8748 (fax)